A CHILD OF SCHOOL AGE

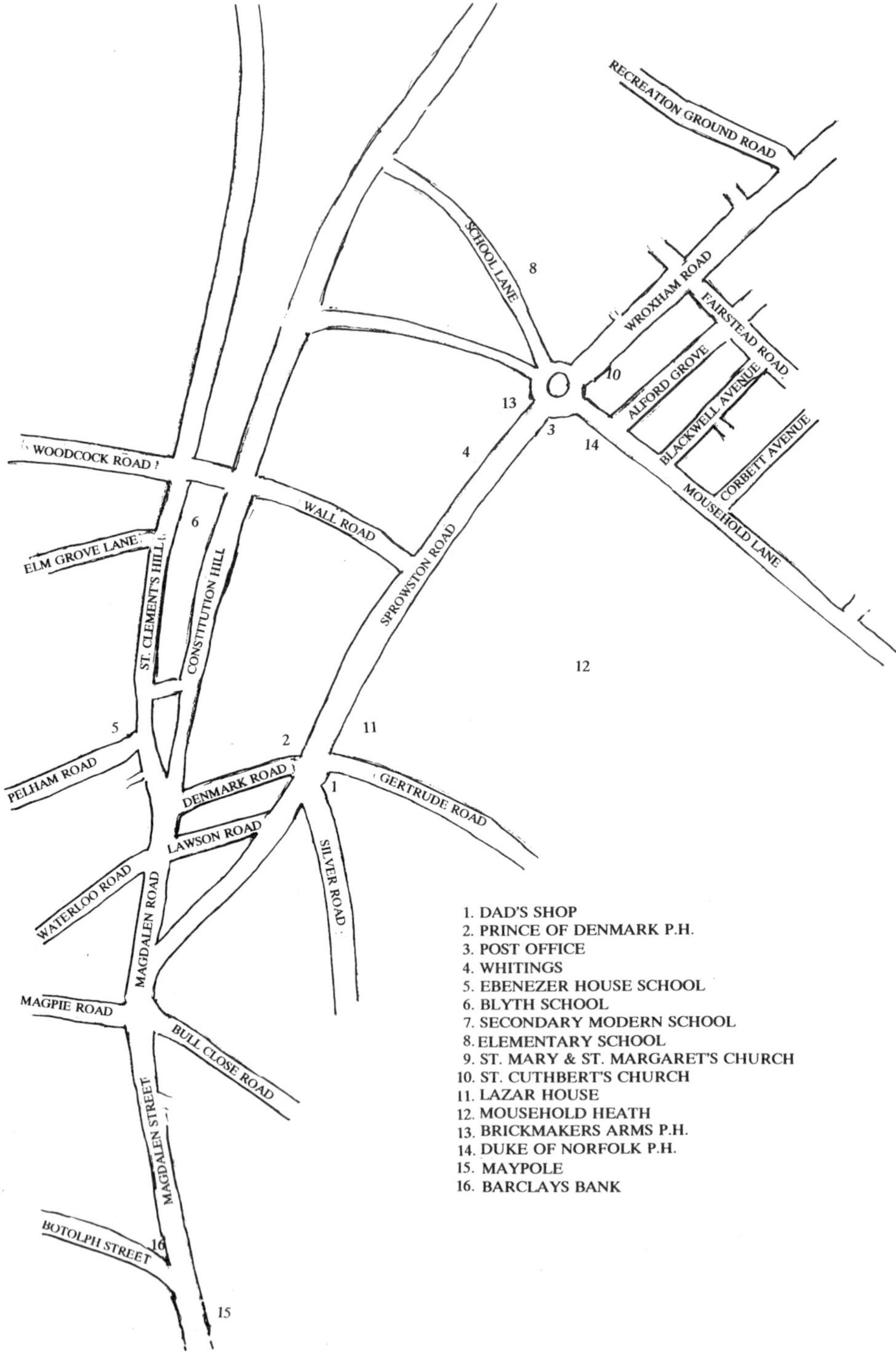
RECREATION GROUND ROAD
SCHOOL LANE
8
WROXHAM ROAD
FAIRSTEAD ROAD
10
ALFORD GROVE
BLACKWELL AVENUE
CORBETT AVENUE
13
3
14
4
WOODCOCK ROAD
WALL ROAD
MOUSEHOLD LANE
6
ELM GROVE LANE
ST. CLEMENT'S HILL
CONSTITUTION HILL
SPROWSTON ROAD
12
5
11
2
PELHAM ROAD
DENMARK ROAD
1
GERTRUDE ROAD
LAWSON ROAD
WATERLOO ROAD
MAGDALEN ROAD
SILVER ROAD
MAGPIE ROAD
BULL CLOSE ROAD
MAGDALEN STREET
BOTOLPH STREET
16
15
1. DAD'S SHOP
2. PRINCE OF DENMARK P.H.
3. POST OFFICE
4. WHITINGS
5. EBENEZER HOUSE SCHOOL
6. BLYTH SCHOOL
7. SECONDARY MODERN SCHOOL
8. ELEMENTARY SCHOOL
9. ST. MARY & ST. MARGARET'S CHURCH
10. ST. CUTHBERT'S CHURCH
11. LAZAR HOUSE
12. MOUSEHOLD HEATH
13. BRICKMAKERS ARMS P.H.
14. DUKE OF NORFOLK P.H.
15. MAYPOLE
16. BARCLAYS BANK

A Child of School Age

Growing up in Norwich 1936-1954

by Brenda Sayle

Author of 'Is This You, Nurse?'

Line drawings by the author

DEDICATION
To the loving memory of my mother and father.

The Larks Press

Typeset and published by
The Larks Press
Ordnance Farmhouse, Guist Bottom,
Dereham, Norfolk NR20 5PF

01328 829207

Printed by the Lanceni Press, Garrood Drive, Fakenham.
March 1997

British Library Cataloguing-in-Publication Data.
A catalogue record for this book is available
from the British Library

Acknowledgements

I would like to acknowledge the help and encouragement given by my family and friends, especially

Miss Diane Sayle
Miss Brenda Muse
Mrs Jean Chamberlain and
Mrs Vivien Riches.

Thanks are also due to Eastern Counties Newspapers and A.E. Coe & Sons Ltd. for permission to use photographs.

© Brenda Copsey 1997

ISBN 0 948400 54 4

Introduction

This account is a result of an interest in family history. Often I have wished ancestors could have left written word of their experiences to shed some light on their lives and times. Conjecture may be far from actuality.

Changes over the last half century have been enormous and continue at an increasing rate. I decided to record my memories for my own family and am happy to share them with others through this book, 'A Child of School Age'.

Aware that there may be some inaccuracies, I sincerely hope they will not spoil the reader's enjoyment when sharing my journey.

March 1997 Brenda Sayle

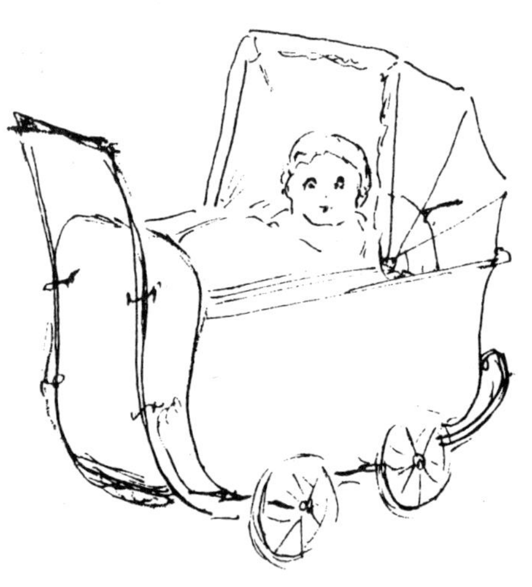

Arrival

The seventeenth of September nineteen hundred and thirty-six was a Thursday. Thursday was half-day closing for the shops in the City of Norwich including my father's shop on the outskirts of the city. Having worked as assistant pharmacist to Mr J.F.Collin at his shop on Gentleman's Walk in the centre of Norwich, my father had decided to open his own pharmacy and in 1933 rented a small lock-up shop on Sprowston Road on land formerly belonging to Denmark Farm and opposite the Prince of Denmark Public House. By the beginning of the century Norwich had spilled through its ancient city walls and smothered the surrounding farmland with hundreds of terrace houses to cope with the rapidly expanding population. The shop was one of four near the tram-sheds of the Norwich Electric Tramways Company between Silver Road and Gertrude Road. The last tram had made its final journey to the tram-sheds and given way to omnibuses which travelled further along the road to Sprowston where, in the 1930s, the small farms and market gardens were also disappearing under bricks and mortar as the need for housing increased again. In Sprowston many of the new dwellings were bungalows and, as my father locked his shop-door that Thursday, he was possibly anticipating a quiet afternoon in the garden of his bungalow in Blackwell Avenue, but Mother and I had different plans! Before he could complete his meal my father was dispatched to '*fetch Nurse*'.

Nurse Lottie Wright lived in Newmarket Street, Norwich, with her beloved brother, George, who had been blinded in World War 1. Nurse Wright had midwifery training and was held in high esteem by doctors and 'mummies' alike. She always called the mothers 'Mummy' and the babies 'wee ones' as she fussed over them and chatted nineteen to the dozen in her gentle Scottish accent. She remained friends with many of her families for the rest of her life, sending birthday cards to her 'wee ones' and bringing silver threepenny pieces for them when she visited. Snowy haired and with soft, lined, pink and white complexion she was a dear!

Mother must have been relieved to see her bustle in, prepared to live as one of the family for as long as necessary, sleeping in the same room as the newly delivered mother and the baby, attending to their every need. Almost four years previously Nurse Wright had delivered my older sister,

Margaret, who had been sent to play with the boy next door whilst I made my entry into the world at a quarter past four that afternoon. When Margaret returned she was told to expect a surprise. Perhaps 'shock' would have been a more appropriate word as, what at first appeared to be a doll lying in the basket-weave cot, gave a very loud cry. The peace had been shattered.

Years later I was to learn that Margaret and I were very different as babies. Whereas Margaret was a 'quiet, dear little baby' I was 'a noisy, long straggly bag of bones'! My redeeming features, according to Mother, were 'big eyes as dark as sloes' which, to my mind, more than compensated for arriving as a long straggly bag of bones.

On my feet and beginning to explore from the age of ten months Mother was in tears and at her wit's end as she told her own mother how I attempted to clamber on to the ironing board when she was ironing or how I had turned on the taps of the gas cooker. Granny's reaction, founded on experience, was,

'Don't worry. They grow up all too quickly. They are not babies for long.'

I cannot actually recall climbing on to the ironing board but I do remember the fascination of the shiny brass taps on the black iron Main gas cooker and the day when Margaret had gone to school and I wanted someone to play with. Suddenly I realised I could open the back door. Marvellous! I hurried down the drive. The gate was open and something exciting was happening on the main road. I ran along the path to watch the men busy with tar and shingle and a big black noisy steam roller.

'Stay there!' the man on the steam roller yelled at me.

'Don't you move!' shouted another.

'Keep still!'

I stood fascinated by all the activity and was just thinking of venturing further when my wrist was grabbed so tightly I could not get free. Mother was red in the face and out of breath after her sprint to catch me. The men shook their heads at me, waved at Mother and carried on working. Mother hurried home, still keeping a tight hold of my wrist.

After that a bolt was put on the back door - high up and well out of my reach.

Supplies

Although there were shops within walking distance many supplies were brought to our back door.

The milk was delivered in bottles by a cheery rosy-faced young man who announced its arrival with a shout of 'whoops!' Some of the dairymen still supplied milk from churns and ladled it into jugs, but ours came in bottles. The bottles had cardboard disc stoppers and these had a smaller central disc which could easily be pushed out. During World War II these discs became much in demand for making shopping bags! Every piece of raffia or string was kept and used to cover the discs, the discs were joined together and handles made from string attached to fashion a strong, attractive useful bag. People produced very imaginative items. 'Whoops' was called up early in the war and our next milkman used a bicycle to make deliveries.

The baker called three times a week and she always had a small dark blue van. In war-time there was little choice of bread and practically no cakes. However, every week, Dad collected a dozen plain buns from another shop. We were lucky to get them but they were incredibly uninteresting. No one would complain and worse was to come when bread was rationed.

Mr Savage who delivered the coal had one of the few lorries in Sprowston. Some, in fact most, of the coal merchants used horses and carts. Mother's diary records that on 3rd November 1939 she received a quarter of a ton of coal at a cost of 13/- which was the *first* of coal rationing. To eke out the coal ration loads of logs were bought from a woodman. The blue paper bags, in which our sugar came, were kept and filled with dampened coal dust before being placed on an established fire. There was a period during one fuel crisis when people were not *allowed* to light fires before 11a.m. It was bitterly cold at the time and we wore our coats, hats and scarves indoors to keep warm. At one time I went to school wearing two vests, a liberty bodice, two blouses, a jumper and two pairs of knickers under my school tunic. It is a wonder I could move! But it was bitterly cold at Miss Bidewell's and every now and then she made us do drill to warm up.

Someone who *always* used a pony and cart was Mr Pointer, the green-grocer. Two or three times a week his old pony would make its slow journey up Mousehold Lane and turn in to Blackwell Avenue. Like us, most of our neighbours grew many of their own vegetables, but Mother usually bought something from the cart. She might grumble if the cabbages had been sampled by too many caterpillars and were full of holes, but these were days before insecticides. Everything was locally grown and definitely during war-time there was no hope of seeing bananas, oranges or grapefruits. But there might be freshly picked peas, runner beans, French beans, marrows, rhubarb, cauliflowers, Fen celery still carrying some of the black fenland soil, parsnips, carrots etc. and, of course, right at the back of the cart, there were always potatoes. In season, lettuces, cos lettuces, tomatoes and cucumbers and fresh fruits, strawberries, raspberries, red, black or white currants and gooseberries and apples, pears or plums. Whether or not all the items were still available by the time Mr Pointer reached us depended on how many people he served en route and sometimes, when he seemed to be taking too long to arrive, Mother would send us out in search of him so she could prepare the vegetables for dinner. Often we helped scrape the new potatoes or shell the peas, sitting outside in the sunshine pressing the pods with our thumbs to open them, then popping the crisp, crunchy peas into our mouths more often than met with Mother's approval! They were nearly as good as the ones we grew in our own garden. After the war Mr Pointer's pony was still hauling the cart around the roads of Sprowston, knowing all his stopping places, and my little sister loved to sit on his back. Then, Mr Pointer became ill and died and another man took on the round but the pony did not want to work for him and the man could not manage the pony and changed to a van before giving up the round altogether and opening a shop. The pony and cart had become history.

Another tradesman calling regularly on us was the laundryman of the Swan Laundry. Because my father wore starched white coats for his work, and because they became soiled by various chemicals, a professional cleaning service was needed, otherwise Mother did all the washing herself, using a gas-heated copper which was concealed under the kitchen draining board. Washday was usually Monday. The copper was filled and heated. In the 'glass-place' an oval zinc bath was placed on a table, filled with water and the pile of dirty linen sorted beside it. The soiled clothes were taken one at a time, soaked, then held against the wash-board, soaped with Fairy Soap and scrubbed before being put in the copper - if they were suitable for the copper, of course, and pushed around with a copper-stick (a thick wooden pole) in the boiling water until clean. Then they were hauled out on the pole and put into cold water in the deep sink for rinsing. Boiled or washed by hand, most of the items were carefully folded ready to be put through the mangle, then hung outside on the line to dry. A blue-bag was swished around in the rinsing water to give the sheets a whiter whiteness. On hot, dry sunny days the sheets were spread flat over the lawn so they dried more quickly. Washdays demanded a lot of organisation and energy and, in my mind, are associated with Housewives' Choice on the wireless, a steamy kitchen, Granny busy at the zinc bath and wash-board with her walking-stick hanging from the table and Mother keeping an ever-watchful eye on me lest I get too close to the boiling water. With luck all would be done and food on the table when Dad came in just after 1p.m.

The zinc bath, cleaned and dried, was hung again on its hook, the packets of Rinso, Oxydol or Persil soap powders returned to the cupboard under the sink, the copper emptied and the draining-board put back in place. It involved such a lot of hard work before the satisfaction of seeing the linen blowing in the breeze. On rainy days it all had to hang in the 'glass-place' and drip as even the best mangling left clothes rather wet. Sometimes the wet washing was hanging around for days.

The next stage in the procedure was, of course, folding and then ironing. When Granny was with us I liked watching her. She did not like using an electric iron but heated her irons by the fire and she tested how hot they were by dipping her fingers in some water and flicking a little on to the base of the iron. She seemed able to judge by the speed the drops shot off. When I had learned how to do French tatting I used up odd bits of wool to make kettle holders for her so she could handle the iron.

There was a time when a mobile library called on a regular basis. It consisted of a few dozen books in the back of a small van. Mother used to borrow from the library man but his enterprise did not survive the war. Later we belonged to the public library at Lazar House, originally a Leper Hospital, on the Sprowston Road near our father's shop. Inside was uncomfortably quiet as no-one was allowed to speak. All the books were covered in dark leather cloth and, apart from the title, their covers gave little indication of the contents. In any case I did not sit still long enough to do much reading.

Early Days

Not everything was delivered to the door and early memories include trips to local shops. I wasted no time when Mother called,

'Come on, Brenda! Get into your pram. We are going to the shops.'

Clutching hold of my inseparable teddy-bear, John Mark, I ran into the lean-to 'glass place' where the low Allwin pram was kept. The 'big' pram was also in there but only used for toys now.

It was a hot, sunny day as we set off at a good speed down Mousehold Lane. Sometimes we went through a little gate along a path between fruit trees to the Post Office just round the corner into Sprowston Road, but not today. We did not stop at the sweet shop either but crossed over to the other side of the road and here Mother paused to look at all the things on the pavement outside Hawes Stores - an emporium of hardware delight. Everything from candles, kindling, cooking pots, saucepans and mousetraps to pan-cleaners, pegs, polish, paint and paraffin could be found there. Mr Hawes, with long thin face and droopy moustache and wearing a buff coloured overall-coat, stood in the doorway enjoying the sunshine. They had a brief conversation then we were off again, slowing as we went up the little 'hill' and gathering speed as we headed down towards Whiting's, butcher's and grocer's shop.

Mother parked my pram outside the shop, I climbed out and, gripping John Mark tightly, managed to get down the steep step into the shop. There was a counter to the right with cotton bags of flour and blue paper bags ready for weighing the sugar. On the floor were potatoes and carrots in wooden bins and . . . . . a cat! As I went to stroke the cat it disappeared behind the curtain separating the shop from the living accommodation and I followed.

The cat ran under a large table but, suddenly self-aware and embarrassed, I found myself looking at an old lady sitting in a large wooden arm chair beside the table. She peered hard at me before asking,

'Were you trying to catch my cat? You won't get him! Look . . .he's hiding right under the table.'

I stood wriggling and uncertain and dare not speak. The old lady suddenly had a bright idea,

'Do you want to *wee*?' she demanded

I stared at her, at her black dress and the shawl around her shoulders, then at the kettle boiling over and spitting on to the fire in the large black iron range, then at the frieze over the mantle shelf and the tub of spills on top. There were big iron tongs, bellows and a long poker and I did not know what to say. The cat, still under the table, started to lick its paw and wash behind its ears but it was keeping an eye on me. Again I started wriggling so the old lady called to her daughter and another lady came into the room.

'Fetch the po!' she ordered, 'The li'le ol' gal wants ter wee!'

A huge chamber pot was placed on the floor near the old lady's chair and I was instructed to pull down my knickers and sit on it. But that was impossible because it was far too big and . . . I fell in! I was still clinging to the rim when Mother's voice asked,

I fell in!

'Where has she got to this time?' And as she came through the curtain a horrified expression appeared on her face and she went redder and redder as she helped me out of the chamber pot.

'I thought she might want to wee,' explained the old lady.

'I think she just wanted to stroke your cat. Thank you.'

The cat sprang silently on to the table and continued cleaning his face with his paw as Mother pulled up my knickers and hurried me out of the shop and into my pram and home.

Daddy laughed when told of our embarrassing moment.

'What is the cat's name?' he asked me, but I did not know and did not want to talk about it. I jiffled on my chair.

'Please may I get down?'

'All right, you may if you have finished your dinner. Say your Grace.'

Putting my hands together and trying to keep my eyes closed I gabbled 'Thank God for-my-good-dinner-please-may-I-leave-the-table?'

Daddy nodded his head and I slid off my chair, picked up John Mark, and ran into the garden. How we loved that garden! In it we played pretence to our hearts' content. Even when alone there was plenty to do, snails, grass-hoppers, bumble bees, bishy-barney-bees (ladybirds) or loopy caterpillars to find. The bumble bees were my favourites as they bumbled and buzzed round the flowers and got lost in the foxgloves.

A few days later I was in the pram again heading up Mousehold Lane to the blacksmith's shop on Salhouse Road. The brake of the pram was broken. Inside the blacksmith's shop it was dark except for the red hot fire and the sparks flying. My nose just reached high enough to satisfy curiosity if I stood on tip-toes.

'She's a nosey-parker I'm afraid.'

'Don't you worry, Ma'am. Let her have a look. I don't suppose I'll be here much longer for her to watch me working.'

The big man took the brake and heated it in the fire. It was bright red when he lifted it out with tongs. He hit it hard with a hammer; sparks flew; it turned dark red. Then he plunged it in to some water. It hissed. He looked at it then said,

'That's done! It will be all right now.'

Mother thanked him, paid him and I got into the pram again.

We had just passed a bungalow, almost hidden in a dip behind some trees on the corner of Corbett Avenue, where I always hoped to see chickens scratching about, when Mother said,

'Here comes the lady who lives there; they are her chickens.'

A lady carrying a basket was coming towards us. She smiled,

'Hello! How are you? I have not seen you for a long time.'

'Hello, Doctor.' Mother said and they started to talk. The lady (*Dr Violet Jewson, who was, I believe, the first woman general practitioner in Norwich*) asked if we were thinking of moving house. She was, and, although she did not really want to leave her beloved 'Mumper's Dingle', she felt it would be safer to live away from the air-fields. After all, she had three children. She looked down at me in the pram.

'How many children have you got now?' she asked.

'Two,' Mother replied. 'The older one is at school.'

'It's difficult to know what to do for the best, isn't it?'

'I think we shall have to stay because of my husband's shop.'

The grown-ups were worried about something and Mother told Daddy about her conversation when he came home for dinner. I could not understand what they were talking about.

Later that summer we went to visit Mother's sisters at Boreham Wood. I have a vague memory of Whipsnade and for the first time seeing an elephant. People were seated high on its back and others were feeding it with buns. I was 'too little' to have a ride. Back at my aunt's house, although not the 'little-est' member of the family as there was a baby cousin in a pram, my cousin and sister would not let me have a turn at being conductor when we played buses in the greenhouse. My 'big' cousin had a conductor's set with a machine and *real* tickets - but I went into a black mood when they declared me 'too little' to be trusted with it. It took an ice-cream to restore harmony. I was often 'too little' for their games and was glad to get home again where I could play with some children of my own age who lived near. They were all boys and, instead of 'mothers and fathers' or 'schools', we played *interesting* games such as making little bricks from clay and baking them hard in the hot sun before constructing walls or bridges with them. I was not to know I was playing with a future physicist who was to work for NASA, but I do know we got marvellously muddy!

More often than not after a day's play in the garden I was made to stand in the deep white porcelain kitchen sink and be washed. From here I could see my sister still in the garden, possibly helping to clear away our play-things, the tea-chests and wooden packing cases which Daddy had brought home from the shop and which we used to make our 'dens'. Although we had a bathroom we could not have baths every day because mains drainage had not reached Sprowston and everyone had to limit the amount of water put down the drains. Having a bath was quite a performance, too, on account of the geyser which heated the water. It was a splendid creation of copper and brass and bore the maker's name E. Ewart and Sons of Coventry. Before the gas jets under the boiler could be lit the cold water input tap was turned on and, when water was flowing out of the spout into the bath, Mother lit the pilot light before turning on the main gas then swivelled it under the boiler and . . 'whoosh'.. all the gas jets lit up and with a loud roar they started to heat the water. Soon hot water was spluttering in to the bath whilst we jumped up and down, laughing at our distorted reflections in the shiny geyser, waiting for the temperature of the water to be checked before being told to get in. It was very exciting, but I believe Mother was always a *little bit scared* of that contraption.

Bathed and dried and in clean pyjamas I stood whilst Mother brushed and plaited my hair, winding rags on the ends in the forlorn hope that the curls produced would prevent ribbons getting lost.

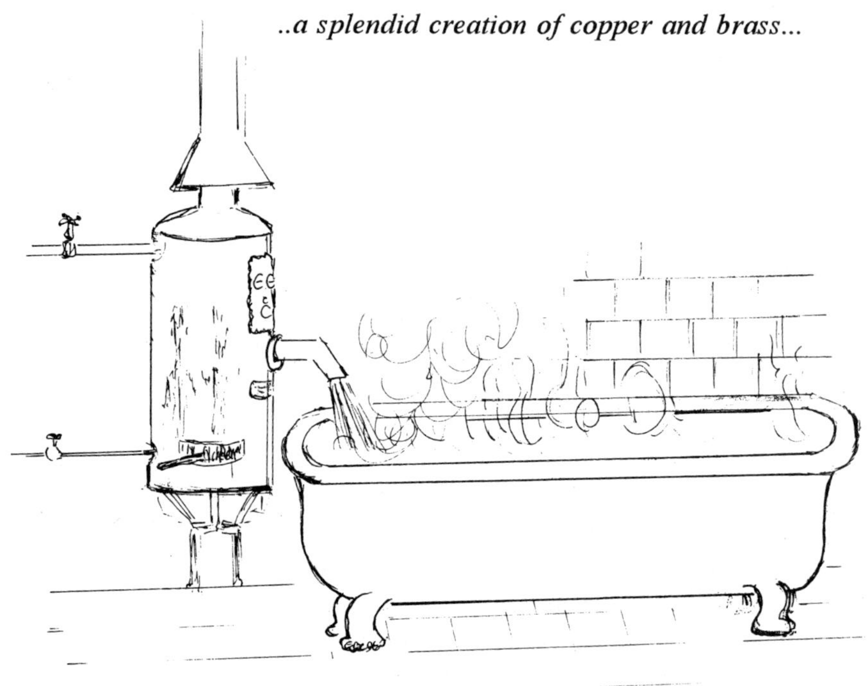

..a splendid creation of copper and brass...

Little Miss 'Lass 'Lace

On our way home from Boreham Wood we went to Huntingdon where Grandfather and Nanny Sayle lived. Their house and shop was an old large rambling property in the High Street and we loved going there. I was crazy to see the animals, the dog, cats, chickens and, in the large stable yard at the back, in the days before the war, horses were stabled. There were some lovely horses, some were race horses, others possibly belonged to people at Cambridge University. There were grooms caring for them and there was a harness room, full of bridles, saddles, straps and all the horsy things. Holding my father's hand he took me with him through the yard to the harness room. A man was stitching a saddle. He looked up as we entered and a smile spread over his face.

'Hello Master Reg!' he said, 'This is a nice surprise. Your father told me you might call in. How are you?"

'Not too badly, thanks. What about yourself?'

'I'm fine - except that I got my calling-up papers this morning.'

'Oh dear!' Daddy shook his head. 'It's a bad job. Let's hope it doesn't take long.'

'How ever long it takes things will never be the same again. The good times are over, Master Reg, and we've had some good times, haven't we?'

'We have. It's a shame . . .'

They talked for a few minutes then Daddy said,

'We must be going. I do hope things are not too bad for you. Good luck.'

'Good-bye, Master Reg. One thing is certain, I won't be here next time you come. I don't know where I'll be.' He shook his head then glanced down at me. 'Take care of your family, and I hope we'll meet again.'

They shook hands. I skipped along beside Daddy as we returned to the house.

'Why did he call you *Master* Reg?'

'He always has done. It's just a little joke.'

'Why won't we see him again?' I asked. 'Why won't he be here next time we come?'

'He has got to go away,' was the reply.

'Where to?'

'We don't know. No-one knows.'

The grown-ups were worried about something and not without good cause. World War Two was not far off.

According to mother's diary, Nurse came to visit us the day before war was declared on Germany. All through the war Mother kept diaries. They were small and without much room for writing but, somehow, she recorded the headline news or items of family interest and they make fascinating reading conveying, as they do, how life went on in those dark days. In some ways our family was lucky. My father suffered from asthma which meant he was unsuitable for active service. He became a member of the Civil Defence. In our front garden a large hole was dug for the Anderson shelter and black-out material was bought for the house windows. We were supplied with gas-masks and, much to my disgust, I was told I was 'too big' to have a Micky Mouse one! Before long we got used to rushing into the shelter when the siren went. Sometimes there had not been time to give an air-raid warning before a crash warning sounded. That meant there was not time to reach the shelter and we went into the windowless hall cupboard instead. This was necessary on July 27th 1941 (according to Mother's diary). I was enjoying myself at the kitchen sink washing doll's clothes whilst Mother was ironing when the crash warning sounded. We could hear the German aeroplane circling overhead. We shot into the hall cupboard. Holding our breath, we clung to each other and Mother prayed to God to save us. The Jerry plane droned round and round then must have dropped the bomb intended for Barnard's engineering works. There was a tremendous bang and we looked at each other with frightened eyes and waited. Soon the all-clear sounded.

'Thank God!'

'God thank,' I echoed Mother's words.

As we went into the back garden to see if there was any damage, our new neighbour looked over the fence. He fetched a brandy for Mother; she was very shaken. There were some tiles smashed above our bedroom. The neighbour climbed a ladder to investigate and managed to bring out a hot piece of shrapnel about 8"x 3"x 1", part of a thousand-pounder sufficient to have killed us if there had not been extra protection installed in the roof above our hall cupboard.

John Mark had, as always, provided me with comfort on that occasion. Already he was beginning to be threadbare especially as I had managed to get hold of some scissors one day and trimmed his fur! Well, my hair had just been cut for the first time and I had been upset to see all the fair curls strewn on the hairdresser's floor. It would help my hair grow thicker I was told and if it did that for mine, why should not John Mark benefit from the same treatment? So my teddy was clipped and, threadbare though he was, nothing else compared to him and I loved him dearly. We had lots of stuffed toys and a few 'hard' dolls which became our 'pupils' when playing schools as we often did. Most of the time they lived in the woven basket cot which had first been mine. There were, however, three old dolls which must have belonged to Mother or to aunts and which spent their days in the hall cupboard. One was a long, gangly thing with staring, painted face and jointed wooden arms and legs, another had once been pretty, but I had pushed its eyes into its china head which still had some hair covering the words 'Made in Germany' and a number on its neck and the third was a broad cloth-bodied doll with hard, flaking painted face and hard hands and feet stuck on to the main body with foul-smelling glue. They were a fearsome trio. Sometimes Margaret and I played wild, frightening games with them, jumping out at each other, brandishing one or other of these terrors. No wonder we had nightmares! Most of the time they were out of sight in the hall cupboard and the door handle was out of my reach. That was fortunate for my younger cousin, Neeta, when she and her mother came to visit one very hot summer's day.

It was really very, very hot and wearing only knickers and sandals I was waiting under the shade of the rowan tree by the front gate in eager anticipation for them to arrive. There was hardly any traffic and sometimes it was just possible to hear the 'bus when its brakes screeched to a halt at The Brickmakers' Arms on Sprowston Road. At last they rounded the corner into Blackwell Avenue and I jumped up and down with delight, but, as they came nearer, Neeta started screaming at the top of her voice and my aunt was having difficulty dragging her along. Mother came hurrying out of the house to see what had happened.

'It's *her!* It's *her* fault!' My aunt pointed an accusing finger at me whilst I tried frantically to hide my head in my knickers. I did not know what I could have done to upset Neeta when she hadn't even arrived. I had been longing for her to come and play.

'What do you mean?' Mother asked. 'She's been standing there as good as gold waiting for you. How can it be her fault?'

'It's her fault!'

'It's those so-and-so dolls!' my aunt shrieked above Neeta's din

I had forgotten all about *those dolls* in the hall cupboard but, evidently, the last time Neeta had come to play we had shut her in the cupboard with them and she had been petrified and had nightmares as a result. With strict instructions from Mother that on no account were we to get the dolls out we managed to persuade Neeta to come indoors. Toffee apples were produced and tears stopped. Then we had a lovely time playing under the hose pipe, dancing in and out of the sparkling rainbow spray. It took my aunt longer to forgive me. Not until she was preparing to leave did I gain her favour. Because when it was time to leave, *Neeta was missing!* High and low we hunted for her. My aunt felt sure I had shut her in the cupboard with those dreadful dolls, but she was found, and it was me that found her, underneath the raspberry net, popping green ones as well as red ones into her mouth as fast as she could! If she had nightmares that night the dolls could not be blamed!

Strawberries rather than raspberries were associated with me for several years. Our new neighbour was a retired greengrocer and a keen gardener. His garden always grew the tallest runner beans, the first potatoes, the biggest marrows, the sweetest peas and lots and lots of strawberries! Every morning I placed my little wicker basket by our dividing wire-netting and every morning kindly Mr P. filled it with juicy red strawberries until, of course, the season came to an end.

'It's no use putting your basket there today,' said Mother one day. 'There won't be any more strawberries this year.'

I felt sure there would be *some* - just a *few*. Full of hope I put my basket there as usual. Later, when I went back to look I was not disappointed. Dear Mr P. must have scoured his plants to find the very last of the crop - small apologies for those earlier succulent beauties. He chuckled as he heard me say to myself,

'Why! There's a little few!' A comment I was never allowed to forget.

That was not the only comment which haunted me throughout my early years, thanks to my Aunt Ida, who was paying us a visit one day when I ran indoors.

'Where have you been?' she asked me.

'In the 'lass 'lace.' I told her

'Where?' she demanded, and started to laugh.

'In the 'lass 'lace.'

Tears trickled down her cheeks as she rocked with laughter and for years she teased me for calling the lean-to *glass place* attached to our kitchen the 'lass 'lace.

'Where are you playing?' she would ask.

'In the 'lass 'lace,' would be my undoubted reply which sent her into near hysterics and from then on she always referred to me as 'Little Miss 'Lass 'Lace'.

A Child of School Age

February 19th 1942 was a Thursday, a gloomy day and the air raid warning had lasted about an hour and a half. It was half-day closing for the shop and Dad was at home but even I knew something was very wrong. There had been worrying news about dear Nanny Sayle. She was extremely ill and Dad had been to Huntingdon the previous Sunday to see her for the last time. Sitting either side of the fireplace in the front room Dad and Mother were talking in sad, subdued tones. They could expect a telegram at any time.

Suddenly someone strode past the bay window and banged with such force on the front door knocker it was a wonder the stained glass did not shatter. It certainly shattered all three of us indoors.

'Whoever is that?' cried Mother, jumping up in alarm.

'I don't know,' Dad replied, puzzled. 'It's not the telegraph boy!'

'I'll go!' And Mother went to open the front door. She was confronted by a large, severe-looking woman wearing a brown tweed costume and a hat with a feather in it and carrying a brown leather brief-case in her kid-gloved left hand.

Before Mother had time to say, 'Good afternoon', a voice boomed,

'I believe you have a child of school age who is not yet attending school?'

'And who am I speaking to?' asked Mother in defensive mode.

'The Education Enforcement Officer,' replied the haughty person.

By this time Dad and I had joined Mother in the narrow hall. I pushed Mother's skirt to one side and peered at the stranger. Her head jerked downwards to look at me.

'Is this the child? Is this Elsie Brenda Sayle?'

I felt uncomfortable. For one thing I was not used to hearing myself called by my first name, Elsie, and it seemed it was I who was the centre of this 'dragon's' attention.

'Yes.' Mother and Dad exchanged glances.

'Then why is she not attending school?' demanded the Inspector. 'I understand she reached her fifth birthday last September.'

'That is correct,' Mother agreed, 'and we are awaiting a vacancy at the school which her elder sister attends. There should be one very soon.'

'There is a perfectly good school down the road, Mrs Sayle! She should go there.'

'She will *not* be going there.'

'Why not?'

'For one thing, we are not happy about the sanitary arrangements. We frequently hear how the little boys make paper boats and sail them on the over-flowing bin lavatories. That thought does not encourage us to consider the school suitable. Besides, we already have made arrangements to send her to a private school with her elder sister. We are very satisfied with that school."

'Which school is that?'

'Ebenezer House.'

'Very well. But remember that if she is not attending school within the month you will be prosecuted!' And the big lady drew herself to her full considerable height, turned on her brogue heels and strode down the drive.

Mother and Dad pulled me away from the door and watched her disappear from sight.

'What about that?' They looked grimly at each other then at me. 'We'll have to ask Miss Bidewell when you can start school.'

'I'll make a cup of tea. We can do with one.' Mother went into the kitchen followed by Dad. They were still shaken by the onslaught.

I picked up John Mark and sat in a corner of the sofa telling him all about it. I didn't think he would be able to come to school with me. I was not at all sure that I *wanted* to go to school.

'It's not the telegraph boy.'

Ebenezer House

On Wednesday 18th March 1942, John Mark had been left sitting in the kitchen arm-chair to 'look after Mother' whilst I was away. Apprehensively I sat in the back of Dad's Standard 9 as we drove to St Clement's Hill. Holding my hand he took me through the small wrought iron gate and up the steep flight of diamond-patterned slate grey steps to the front door of No.2 Pelham Road. The door of Ebenezer House School was opened by Miss Florence Bidewell.

I had met Miss Florence Bidewell before. She was small and thin with white hair, beady brown eyes behind tortoiseshell-rimmed spectacles, and a one-sided smile which just showed a chipped tooth on a dark-red dental plate. This plate was a bit loose so it made an intriguing clacking sound from time to time and the chipped tooth provided a whistle to accompany 'sh' sounds; all fascinating to a five-year old and a distraction during lessons.

Ebenezer House School had been founded before the turn of the century by Miss Florence Bidewell's elder sister, Grace. Miss Florence had joined the school in 1908. Their sister, Katie, also taught there. Special teacher training was not required at that time and none of them were trained but took up teaching as soon as they left school. They had all been educated at private schools in the city of Norwich.

Miss Florence Bidewell told how their first pupils wore frilled pinafores and button boots and the boys had long hair and wore velvet suits. By the time I arrived there was a uniform, introduced in 1926 as a concession to the new era of education. It was black and heliotrope - not purple or mauve but *heliotrope!* It consisted of a black tunic or gym-slip and a black raincoat. The black velour hat had a black and heliotrope hat-band. The black blazer had, white and

She was small and thin.

heliotrope braid stitched carefully round the edge. There were grey knee socks held up by garters, and indoors we had to wear black plimsolls. Perhaps at one time the jumpers were of heliotrope, but I remember grey ones. In summer we wore dresses, preferably heliotrope, and panama hats with elastic, of course, under the chin to keep them in place. Under our gym-slips we wore black, fleecy-lined bloomers with a handkerchief pocket, a vest and liberty bodice. During the war-time uniform restrictions were less rigid because of the difficulty of obtaining anything let alone items of the correct type and colour. However, most of the mothers did their best to comply. The number of children at the school was usually about twenty to twenty-five.

That first morning, after a few words with my father, Miss Bidewell told Margaret to take me to the cloakroom. We went along the narrow track between the privet hedge and the house, across the shingle-covered area, which would have been the back garden if this had not been a school, and in through the back lobby. On the right was the lavatory, the door slightly ajar, small squares of old newspapers tied together with string hanging on a nail for use as toilet paper just as in most other lavatories during war-time. On the left the back door was open. We passed through the tiny kitchen with its shallow, yellow earthenware sink and gas stove into the cloakroom. Several children had arrived already and turned to stare at the newcomer. I was shown where to hang my coat and gas-mask and one of the older girls helped tie the laces of my plimsolls. My sister held my hand and pulled me towards the door of the next room which was our classroom. We stood on the coconut mat. Miss Bidewell was teaching someone at the piano. When she turned to look at us Margaret said 'Bonjour, Miss Bidewell,' and received the reply, 'Bonjour, Margaret. Bonjour Brenda.' This, presumably, justified the 'Conversational French' on their prospectus .

In the centre of the room was a big oblong table and children were collecting their exercise books from the large bookcase by the wall. Each had their own particular place. The little ones sat on a form along one side of the table; from there they progressed to seats at either end and the older children sat on chairs. Margaret sat on one of the chairs along one side whilst I was instructed to sit on the very end of the form. That meant everyone else had to squeeze up and the one on the other end almost fell off! Eventually we had settled down quietly. The other children stared at me and I felt myself blushing but soon Miss Bidewell had them all busy

'Bonjour, Miss Bidewell.'

doing arithmetic. Then Miss Bidewell brought a chair and sat beside me.

'I want you to show me if you know your letters,' she said. In front of me was placed a copy of Chambers' First Primer. We had one at home and Margaret had tried to teach me when we played schools with our toys.

o c e
s a
i j
k h l
b d p q
m n

and so on. The letters most resembling each other were grouped together and we soon learned to recognise them in print and make the appropriate sounds. The next page was short sentences of two-letter words.

'It is in'
'He is on'

Then to the three-letter words,

'The cat sat on the mat'

And four letter words

'The lass sits on the moss' or something similar.

Much to Miss Bidewell's delight I could read to that level. Margaret was praised for her teaching efforts.

Everyone around the table received individual attention.

There was mid-morning break and a queue for the lavatory, although that did not stop frequent requests of 'Please may I leave the room?' throughout the day.

'Do not forget to wash your hands,' was the constant reminder after such a request was granted. But the thin, grey, smelly roller-towel by the kitchen sink probably spread more germs than unwashed hands might have done. While we washed our hands with the little piece of hard Sunlight soap and waited to dry them, Miss Bidewell was also in the kitchen preparing her lunch. In a small saucepan on the gas she boiled celery. Possibly she ate the celery for her evening meal because it was only the celery *water* which she had at lunchtime with a piece of bread or toast. She told us celery was good for rheumatism. Maybe that was how she continued to ride her upright bicycle well into her seventies!

Refreshed from being outside in the open air we returned to our places. Now we recited our 'Times Tables'. All together we chanted from 'once two is two' through to 'twelve twelves are a hundred and forty-four'. Under the table our legs had been swinging with the beat and did not stop still until we arrived breathless and triumphant at that final number. It was a long time before I realised that multiplication was a form of addition and that, if I was quick enough, I could use my fingers under the table to make sure of the next number. The one which confused me was after seven sevens are forty nine, eight sevens are . . . and nine sevens are . .? I was all right when we got to ten sevens are seventy. That was easy. But where did sixty-three come in? Oh! there it was again when we did our nine times table at seven nines! Gradually the daily repetition fixed it in our memories.

In the same way, day after day we chanted through the Kings of England.

'William the Conqueror Ten-sixty-six to ten-eighty-seven
William the Second 1087 to 1100
Henry the First 1100 to 1135
Stephen 1135 to 1154'

and on and on we went through history, swinging our legs under the table and arriving at

'Edward the Eighth..... Abdicated!' glad of the change of rhythm and ending proudly with

'George the Sixth 1936'.

We had reached our own time! George the Sixth was *our* King. It was in the name of King George of England, Scotland and Northern Ireland and the Empire that our soldiers, sailors and airmen were fighting to keep our country free. We were very aware that our country was at war with Germany. In Katie Bidewell's classroom a Morrison Air-raid shelter served as the table and, if there was not time to get across St Clement's Hill to the public air-raid shelters under Sewell Park when the warning siren wailed, we all dived into the Morrison. It was a squash in there and one of the boys suffered from asthma, so there was always a lot of shuffling round until he was near the opening.

On the wall was a large map of the world, much of it coloured pink. The pink parts were *ours*. They were *Empire*. We did Geography on Wednesdays. Wednesday also was the day for 'colouring'. I loved colouring, but paper and crayons were in desperately short supply due to the war. On the table, grooved by generations of children running their pencil points along the grain of the wood, a wooden box containing pencils and crayons was placed centrally in reach of all. The utility pencils, without any pretty covering, were horribly chewed. Only the 'big' children were allowed to use the *pencil* crayons. The 'little ones' had to make do with the broken points or the messy war-time wax crayons. The big children were sometimes allowed to paint with water-colours.

My first day at school was a Wednesday but, until then, Wednesday afternoons had been when I went to dancing class. At No.1 Fairstead Road Miss Loveless taught dancing; Greek, Ballet and Ballroom. Margaret had lessons on a Saturday but I went with the little ones on Wednesday afternoons and had shown some promise according to Miss Loveless. Because of this I was given permission by Miss Bidewell to have Wednesday afternoons off school for the time being and was allowed to do my colouring during the morning. Promising or not, my dancing did not last long because, one day, another girl, a 'botty little thing', jealous when the teacher praised me, suddenly pinched and twisted the flesh on my upper arm until it hurt dreadfully. I refused to go again. Soon after, the classes stopped because of the war.

Games

Obviously the war affected our lives at school in all sorts of ways. There were shortages of *everything*, not only of paper and crayons. On Mondays we had scripture in the mornings and sewing or embroidery in the afternoons. As the war progressed, obtaining silks and cottons was almost impossible. Miss Bidewell occasionally cycled down to Tombland to the little shop bearing the name *Olive Mann* in gold-leaf on the brown fascia above the door. Inside, Miss Mann kept her stock of Anchor silks and whatever canvasses or materials she could get, determined to continue in business despite Hitler's bombs. Greatly prized crewel needles and Anchor silks and even the poorer war-quality cottons were carefully stored by Miss Bidewell in a big box on the top shelf of the classroom bookcase. Wasting nothing, Miss Bidewell wound any useful length around lace bobbins which, she told us, had belonged to her mother. Also on the top shelf were about eight wooden dowels which had belonged to her father whom, she claimed, was one of the few men who had completed the exhausting 'Norfolk Long Dance'. We used the dowels when we attempted the 'Sword Dance' or 'Scottish Dancing', but no Scot would have recognised what *we* were doing!

Friday afternoons was set aside for such activities which were included in 'Drill'. The big table was moved to one side of the room and we spaced ourselves as best we could. To start with we clapped our hands 'in front, behind, in front and above', repeating this exercise many, many times then we might sit on the floor, each child between the open legs of another, hands on the shoulders of the one in front and swaying rhythmically to 'And so we float in a golden boat, far away, far away.' Standing up again we attempted to touch our toes and stretch our hands down the sides of our legs as far as we could. There really was not room for much else. Then it was time for prayers before changing our plimsolls for out-door shoes, putting on our coats, hats, scarves and gloves, picking up our gas-masks and rushing outside to our waiting parents. No doubt the walk home was better physical exercise than anything we did in the classroom.

Whilst the advertised curriculum included 'Drill' there was no pretence of teaching 'Games'. There was definitely no room for games. There was scarcely room for play-time outside.

On the small shingle-covered patch behind the house we played 'pig-in-the-middle', 'the farmer's in his den', 'what's the time Mr Wolf?' and 'statues' or 'chocolate', although there was no chocolate to reward the winner as sweets were rationed, of course. Sometimes we were allowed in to the passage-way outside the back gate to do skipping, but ball games were not advisable as the neighbour complained when they went *over* the wall and Miss Grace Bidewell complained at the noise *on* the wall. Miss Grace Bidewell no longer taught and was frequently unwell. It was her need for quiet which put an end to us playing what must have been an ancient game passed down through many generations. It was called 'The King of the Barbareens'. To play it one of the boys was chosen to be king and he selected a 'messenger'. The rest of the children pretended to be busy working in fields until the king sent his messenger to demand their surrender whereupon they shouted, 'We won't surrender! We won't surrender!' and 'Go tell the King! Go tell the King! The King of the Barbareens!' and the messenger replied, 'I'll tell the King! I'll tell the King! The King of the Barbareens!' and the messenger went to the King who was very angry and sent his messenger to catch someone. The 'mob' did not know who had been selected and there was a skirmish as the messenger pounced and carted the chosen prisoner to the king. Of course, the prisoner tried to escape and the messenger was sent to make more captures and there were more shouts of 'We won't surrender! We won't surrender!' It could become a very noisy game indeed.

'The King of the Barbareens'

When free school milk was introduced we drank our third of a pint through waxed paper straws which soon became unwound, soggy and useless. They were nowhere near as good as the *real* wheat straws had been, but those were no longer obtainable. On warm days the milk did not taste very nice but Miss Bidewell insisted we must not waste it. Of course she did not have a refrigerator. Few people did.

Indoors on rainy or snowy days we sat in the cloakroom and played Chinese whispers after those of us who could not get home had eaten our packed lunches.

I was a 'pingler' and Mother was hard-pressed to think of food to put in my box. She cut the bread very thinly and spread it with as much butter as the ration would allow. Rations had been introduced in January 1940, four months after the outbreak of the war, and were strict but fair as they applied to everyone. Amounts allowed varied from time to time but to start with each person's weekly ration consisted of 4 ounces of butter, 12 ounces of sugar, and 4 ounces of bacon *or* ham. By July tea was also rationed to 2 ounces per week, as was cooking fat or margarine. Meat was limited by price, each adult being allowed 1/10 worth per week with only 11d. worth for children under six years old - so I could not expect roast beef sandwiches! Instead I had apple and brown sugar sandwiches or lettuce, sprinkled with white sugar in sandwiches, corned-beef or spam sandwiches and, occasionally, a fresh egg to boil and some bread and butter. Miss Bidewell let us boil eggs on her gas stove. Sometimes there might be a home-made bun or piece of cake - if the rations had stretched that far that week. And, because we had apple trees in our garden, there most likely would be an apple, but no chance of there being a banana in anyone's box because they were not obtainable and oranges were few and far between. One of the boys sometimes had *dried* bananas but they could not portray what real bananas looked like and not many of us could remember *those*, so we had to wait until after the war to sample them and, when they did eventually arrive in the greengrocers', grown-ups teased us because we did not know how to get into them!

It is doubtful that we felt *deprived* in any way and we knew that, in war-time, there were shortages; no one must be greedy and nothing wasted. Any garden produce which could be stored or preserved was stored or preserved. Apples were picked, sorted and wrapped in newspaper before being packed into wooden crates; potatoes were dug up and put into hessian

Waiting for our eggs to boil

sacks; onions hung up in a cool shed; carrots put under sand; eggs carefully placed in a large earthenware crock and covered with water-glass to seal them; pounds of runner beans were picked, sliced and salted down in another big crock and kept in the pantry. Fruits which could be bottled were bottled, although on some occasions the correct temperature cannot have been maintained for the correct length of time and, after a few days or weeks we were dismayed to find fermentation had started and the suspect jars were carefully placed outside before they exploded! Other fruits were turned into jam and, I believe, extra sugar was granted on top of the usual ration for that purpose. And, of course, there were pickles and chutneys.

People whose gardens produced more than they needed were often willing to let others, especially those with children, have any surplus. Across the road from our bungalow were two semi-detached bungalows with long back gardens. As a very little girl I remember going with Mother to visit a retired teacher in one of these. Miss Blaxter was quick to realise my 'jiffling' on Mother's lap was due to boredom and she placed some brilliants on her polished table next to her Bible, writing paper, pen and ink and spots of rainbow danced around the walls and ceiling in the morning sunshine. I was fascinated. I liked Miss Blaxter. As I grew older I went alone to see her and help her pick raspberries and redcurrants whilst Margaret picked blackcurrants in another garden.

Photo: E. Johnson Taylor

The Sayle family in 1938

1940 - Brenda with John Mark

1942 - Ready for school
Ebenezer House

Photo: Eastern Evening News

My father, E. Reginald Sayle, Pharmacist, on his retirement. December 1972.

195a Sprowston Road, Norwich.

The Standard 9

The former Ebenezer House Preparatory School, photographed in 1986.

The Notre Dame Convent and Preparatory School (from a 1920s postcard).

A classroom at Notre Dame Preparatory School, Norwich (from a 1920s postcard).

Notre Dame High School entrance.

1952 Ready for school
Notre Dame

Next to Miss Blaxter lived an elderly couple, Mr and Mrs B. and, when Mother was desperately short of eggs, we were sent with stale bread, kitchen peelings and cabbage leaves for their chickens in the hope that they could spare one or two for us. Standing on the steep step we knocked on the back door which was opened by a tiny, bent lady with snowy white hair in a small bun who gladly accepted our offerings for her hens. Told to walk through the garden to find Mr B. I went along the path between fruit bushes until I caught sight of Mr B's ancient, greasy trilby hat, brim turned down all round, bobbing about, almost hidden by giant rhubarb leaves. Bright blue eyes in rosy, weather-worn cheeks turned to look at me. A stub of hand-rolled cigarette drooped from his mouth beneath a bushy, singed moustache. He took me to the hen house, looked in the nest boxes and found eggs, still warm, which he placed carefully in my little basket. The chickens made contented clucking sounds as they scratched newly dug earth and found worms. I stayed as long as possible watching them and the rabbits, silently twitching their noses, in nearby hutches. Some of the rabbits would supplement the meat ration no doubt, but one was *always* there, an enormous 'cushion' of brown fur with long floppy ears. Then, thanking Mr and Mrs B., I hurried home to Mother with the eggs.

We were, fortunately, never really hungry and Mother was a good cook of straightforward, wholesome foods. (*British foods, of course, as foreign foods like pasta and curry did not 'invade' our kitchens until after the war when people were free to travel and immigrants introduced their culinary customs.*) Sometimes, our tummies rumbled and we might rush in to the kitchen to discover what was for dinner only to get the answer,

'Laroes for meddlers!'

'What do you mean?' Mother chuckled at our puzzled faces.

'What I say,' she laughed. '*Laroes for meddlers* and *you'll* be the first!' We ran off as she pretended to try and catch one of us.

It was a saying meaning something like, 'Don't poke your nose in or you'll get a slap on your bottom!' It also meant, 'Wait and see!' as far as our dinner was concerned, so we carried on playing.

On cold winter days many an hour was spent toasting bread on a toasting fork in front of a red hot fire, getting scorched oneself in the process. Another treat, especially after playing outside in the snow, was to come in to the kitchen and discover that Mother was roasting onions on the fire. Large onions were perched on the grate at the edge of the fire to cook.

Carefully they were turned round with the tongs then, when cooked through, they were lifted on to old newspapers where the burned outer layers were removed. Then Mother put them on our plates with a knob of butter and they were *delicious*.....and all the more so because of the fun and uncertainty of getting them as they sometimes fell into the fire and were lost!

And that reminds me of a fall I had, not into a fire, although the burning pain was *excruciating*. It was when Granny was living with us and Mother had gone in to Norwich to do some shopping. Granny was busy preparing vegetables in the kitchen when I went down the garden and saw lovely blackberries ripe in the hedge. The only problem was the heap of stones under the hedge. As we lived near Mousehold Heath the land was very, very stony and, over the years, many had been removed from the vegetable plot and thrown under the hedge. However the temptation was great and I climbed up the pile of stones but, just as I reached the blackberries, the scree gave way and I slid rapidly down the slope and straight into a bed of stinging nettles! Never will I forget that pain! My legs were covered in nettle stings and I did not know what to do because, no doubt, I had been told to 'Be a good girl. Don't worry Granny.' When Mother came home she found me still trying to take the heat out with cold water. Only then did I start to cry. Granny had not realised I was hurt and, if only I had sought her help, *she* would have known what to do. There were dock leaves growing next to the stinging nettles as they often do.

Granny knew remedies for almost everything. She had brought up her six children in the days when people *managed* without rushing to the doctor or chemist. One of her cures was a favourite of mine when I had a cough - it was butter, brown sugar and vinegar pills. Nice . . and very effective! And thinking of those pills reminds me of other medicaments used on us, for example camphorated oil rubbed on to our chests before we went to bed to ease our breathing when we had colds; Sayle's Bronchial Mixture for Children for coughs; syrup of figs for constipation and glycerine suppositories if that failed! Golden Eye Ointment for styes on eyes, which I got frequently especially when we slept in the dug-out. Toothache was eased with Tincture of Myrrh or Bunter's Nervine; a few drops of warmed olive oil gently put into the ears for earache; witch hazel worked wonders on bruises and T.C.P. was dabbed on stings and bites although vinegar might be used on wasp stings and the washday 'blue bag' on bee stings.

Lessons

Throughout the four years I spent at Ebenezer House the time-table never varied. Every day we chanted times tables and the monarchs from William the Conqueror. Every day we did sums and reading and learned to write in our copy-books. At first we practised up-strokes and down-strokes, making 'pot-hooks' and 'cup-hooks', laboriously guiding our pencils between the double lines printed on the page as we copied the text above, 'Whatever is worth doing is worth doing well,' or 'The quick brown fox jumps over the lazy dog.' When we had mastered the small letters we moved on to twirly capitals some of which were extraordinarily difficult. Miss Bidewell demonstrated using her pen and ink, making sure she had a good Waverley nib in place before dipping it carefully into the Stephen's blue-black ink. It would be some years before we were allowed to use ink and we had to be content with the short bits of horribly chewed pencils impressed 'HB WAR DRAWING.' Miss Bidewell sometimes referred to the pencils as 'cedars' but the ones we used were not made from cedar wood, they were soft and the leads inside broke easily. All our work was in pencil and it was better not to make any mistakes because the paper in our exercise books was of such poor quality that it tore as soon as we tried to rub out.

On Tuesdays the special subject was History. Our textbooks were ancient and with only a few black and white illustrations. One very grey day under a low-powered electric light what happened during the lesson is vividly etched in my memory. I must have been about seven at the time because I had progressed to one of the stools at the end of the table. We all sat with history books in front of us - not the same books as each other as we were all at different stages. Miss Bidewell came to each one of us in turn, listening to our reading. I was very bored having to hear stories I had already been through myself and my own story on this particular day was 'horrible'. Not long having acquired the skill to read quietly to myself I had looked at the page - and read it. There was a picture on the opposite page showing the arrow entering Harold's eye. My imagination ran riot! I felt sick. Suddenly Miss Bidewell moved her stool and sat beside me.

'Now Brenda, read your piece for today.'

'I've read it already,' I mumbled.

'No you have not. I want to hear you read it.'

'No! I do not want to read it. I *have* read it! I read it to myself.' I could not bear to read that dreadful story again.

'Come on. I want to *hear* you read it.'

'No!' I said defiantly. I do not suppose I had ever previously felt so angry and then Miss Bidewell moved nearer and touched the book. Suddenly I could not bear her near me and I clenched my fists, plunging them with all my strength into her chest. She toppled backwards on her stool, almost falling to the floor. Shocked, she stood up and made me take my stool and sit apart from those at the table. Red in the face I sat subdued with my back to the other children and stared at the miserably small coal fire which was the only source of heat. There were never more than two or three coals on the fire. I watched the weak flames disappear into the smoke up the chimney until it was time to go home. Undoubtedly my parents were told of my misbehaviour, but nothing was made of it and, as the episode was out of character, was probably attributed to my being tired after a night of air-raids and broken sleep. Apart from the arrow entering Harold's eye the only other History lesson I remember concerned King John's jewels being lost in the Wash. It is doubtful all of us realised the Wash did not refer to Monday washday though!

It is even more difficult to recall our geography lessons, apart from the world map pinned to the wall and on which Miss Bidewell pointed out places where Germans were marching across Europe. It was very frightening and we were glad to see the Straits of Dover between us and the Continent. The fathers of some of the children were soldiers fighting in Europe or the Far East and some, of course, never returned. Some were in the Royal Navy or in the Merchant Navy and we were frequently reminded of the hazards such brave men faced when, for instance, bringing our food and various supplies across the Atlantic Ocean. We must *never* waste any of our food. The flat pale blue representation of sea on the wall map could not possibly convey the huge seas tossing the ships, the horrors of torpedoes and men drowning. We were spared the reality of television and grown-ups, on the whole, did not enlighten us as to the latest news and I can remember my mother being disgusted on one occasion when Miss Bidewell had told of some dreadful atrocities. At home we were usually in bed before the nine o'clock news although sometimes we stayed to hear the reassuring chimes of Big Ben and the voice of the newsreader, John Snagge or Alvar Lidell, who was my favourite. As the war progressed we learned of pilots like Guy

Gibson and Douglas Bader and tried to visualise what it must be like to be a prisoner-of-war. Vivid imaginations meant we all had nightmares at some time. We needed vivid imaginations to picture geographical features such as water-falls and volcanoes. Even mountains were regular conical shapes in our minds' eye as Miss Bidewell described them. She, presumably, had never actually seen one herself so was unable to be more explicit.

Her descriptions of stories from the Bible were more elaborate and we learned of Adam and Eve to Noah and the Good Samaritan and the Raising of Lazarus from the dead, amongst others. The story of Lazarus troubled me for some time and, when word circulated that the Vicar of a nearby church had collapsed in front of his congregation and died, I dare not look when we passed the church the following day in case his body was still stretched out on the path!

Mention of Adam and Eve reminded the children, especially some of the boys, of the riddle,

'Adam and Eve and Nip-me-tight went down the river to bathe,
Adam and Eve got drowned. Who do you think was saved?'

They chanted this as they pranced around the unwary and were delighted when given the answer they sought. It was very much a case of 'Once nipped, twice shy!' And Miss Bidewell had her own ways of dealing with children who tormented others or who misbehaved or talked too much during lessons. A boy who shocked Miss Katie Bidewell by his rudeness to her was sent into our classroom for punishment by Miss Florence. In the corner he was made to stand for a long time holding a very heavy book, possibly a Bible, above his head. We began to feel sorry for him as his face grew redder and redder and his knees began to wobble.

His knees began to wobble

Blitz

Just over a month after I started school, the City of Norwich suffered the Blitz. Norwich would never be the same again.

During the night of Monday 27th April 1942 Norwich was heavily attacked. Woken from our sleep by the wail of the siren, we hurried out to the Anderson shelter. The action was over the city rather than over us, and for a time we watched the searchlights circling, trying to pick out the German fighters and bombers, we heard the shell fire and the sky was red as buildings went up in flames. It was exciting yet horrifying, and worrying to think that some of our relations were in it, somewhere.

Mother was very anxious and, in the morning, asked Dad if he had sufficient petrol left to make the journey across the city. Fortunately he had and set out to see how things were. Granny, Grandfather and Auntie Joyce were shaken but safe. He suggested they came to ours for a while but, although there had been much devastation, they said they would stay in their own home. That night everything was quiet, but Mother was uneasy and on the Wednesday managed to persuade them to come to sleep at ours. Granny placed small packets on the kitchen table. Their rations. A few ounces of butter, margarine, cheese, tea and sugar to last them overnight. I can still visualise those little packs of essentials sitting on the table-cloth. That night the German raiders were back again. From our dug-out we heard the battle, the sky glowed bright red once more, the searchlights scanned and pin-pointed the attacking planes and we held our breaths as we watched. Was *anything* left of Norwich? Was the *Cathedral* still there?

In the morning Grandfather, a master carpenter, got ready for work. As he strapped leather buskins on his legs and hung the large tool-bag on the cross-bar of his big upright bicycle he told Granny he would try to find out what had been hit during the raids. First, though, he must get to work.

Evidently, as soon as he got there, he heard someone say,

'They caught a packet in Somerleyton Street last night.'

He was given permission to go and discover just how big a packet. It must have been a terrible sight for him. He returned to ours as soon as he could and his face was grim. Heavily he got off his bike and came indoors. He looked at Granny and, with tears in his eyes, he said hoarsely,

'It's all gone, Ethel. It's all gone.' He sank down on to a chair.

Mother fetched the small bottle of brandy kept for emergencies.

Granny, Grandfather and Auntie Joyce lived with us for eighteen months during which time they slept in the house and we slept down the dug-out. Auntie Joyce, Mother's youngest sister, worked in an office in Norwich. She was a member of the Civil Defence before being conscripted into the A.T.S. early in 1944.

No photograph exists to record the scene in Somerleyton Street as, even if Dad had had one of the rarely obtainable films, ordinary citizens were not allowed to photograph war damage, presumably in case it could be misused by the enemy as propaganda.

I was with Mother when she went to look at the rubble which had been the little house where she had spent much of her childhood. Sadly thoughtful, we stood holding hands looking at the devastation. A few pieces of corrugated iron lay where the chicken-house had been.

'Where are the chickens?' I wanted to know.

Mother shook her head.

A black and white cat with staring green eyes sat on a dustbin near to where Granny's line-post stood at a crazy angle.

'Is that Tibbles?' I asked. It did not look *quite* like Tibbles but hopefully . . .

'No. That's not Tibbles, I'm afraid,' came the reply.

'Where do you think Tibbles is?'

I looked up at Mother. She was shaking her head and was near to tears.

'Thank God they were with us that night,' she said quietly and gave my hand a reassuring squeeze.

If they had not been with us that night Granny, Grandfather and Auntie Joyce would have gone the same way as the chickens and Tibbles.

As Grandfather had said,

'It's all gone. It's *all gone*.'

'No that's not Tibbles.'

Music

I did *not* like school. The expression on my face every morning was sufficient for the grown-ups to realise that fact. With gas-mask slung across my shoulder and holding Margaret's hand I walked miserably up the avenue then turned to wave to Mother and Granny before we rounded the end of the privet hedge in to Mousehold Lane. Once there, my sister pulled me along faster than I could run and then let go of my hand and went ahead, hurrying along past the houses and the big oak trees of the vicarage garden. She *loved* school! The branches of the trees stretched right across the road to touch the trees on the other side. Their trunks were banded with white paint so they showed up in the dark now that no lights were allowed. I could just remember the lamp-lighter cycling along pulling on the gas-lamps but my only thought on our way to school was - *would my sister wait for me?* I was petrified she might leave me behind, but she had been given strict instructions and duly waited for me to cross the big road with her. Then she ran ahead again and joined the usual queue at the 'bus stop.

Evidently, I was not the only one to feel miserable on school days because watching us set out with me obviously so miserable ruined the mood of the morning for Mother and Granny too.

'Whatever are we going to do about her? I don't think I can bear it much longer.' Mother turned her worried gaze towards her own mother.

'You can't do anything. She's got to go. She'll get over it.' And Granny changed the subject. 'Shall we make a start on the washing?'

I wonder what Granny's thoughts really were. She, herself, had suffered teasing at school because she was lame. As a little girl she had fallen down stairs and lay unconscious. When she eventually came round it was discovered that her foot had been hurt. She was taken to the hospital where a doctor operated and cut the tendons so that her foot never grew and she had little schooling. That was a great shame because she had a quick, lively brain and she would have done well.

Fortunately, shortly before the Blitz, the upright Broadwood piano which had been in the front room of Granny's house came to ours and Margaret and I started piano lessons with Miss Bidewell. Every morning we had about ten minutes tuition before the start of school. Ten minutes was enough for players and listeners alike.

The piano, draped with a faded blue dust-sheet, stood in the corner near the fireplace. Even when the fire was alight the warmth from it was insufficient to thaw our fingers on a cold day but not all the days were cold, of course. Miss Bidewell sat on a stool slightly behind her pupil counting 'one-two-three, one-two-three' or whatever the timing might require.

Counting one-two-three....

On top of the piano were piles of music scores, books of studies, hymns and songs. Songs? O yes, we had singing lessons and amongst the songs I remember learning were :-

The Londonderry Air; Killarney; O the Days of the Kerry Dancing!; The Cornish Floral Dance; Cherry Ripe

and towards Christmas,

Hail, Smiling Morn; Nazareth; and Hark the Herald Angels amongst others.

The sounds of no more than a dozen 5 - 10 year-olds squeaking their best rendering of such pieces must have been painful to hear, but Miss Bidewell trilled away,

'O the days of the Kerry Dancing, O the ring of the piper's tune,
O for one of those hours of gladness, Gone, alas, like our youth, too soon!'

Her back straight, her arms stretched out to the key-board, her beady brown eyes shining, she turned to look at us every now and then as she sang; her teeth clacked and whistled and she sprayed us with a fine spray of saliva. I can see her clearly in my memory and clearly she enjoyed her singing.

Her enjoyment of music resulted in an annual Musical Evening to which parents and friends were invited. All were welcomed at the front door by children taking it in turns to practise their French,

'Bon soir, Madame!' and 'Bon soir, M'sieur!' giving a little curtsey or bow as they did so, then taking them to a seat ready for the performance.

Not all the items were musical as not all the children took music lessons. There were recitations and sometimes it was necessary to dress up as I did on one occasion to recite, 'Little Miss Muffet'. In a green taffeta dress, which had belonged to an aunt, and large, red straw hat I sat on a 'tuffet', (a low stool) and said my verse, pulling on a thread to encourage from its hiding place a large woollen spider with button eyes and eight wire legs to come and sit down beside me! *That* surprised the smaller children and caused a few squeals of mock horror.

One year, after I had left the school but continued my music lessons with Miss Bidewell on Saturday mornings, the Annual Musical Evening was a much grander affair. Miss Bidewell decided her house was no longer big enough for the event and hired a local church hall. Incredibly a copy of the programme survives and shows names of the pupils, some of whom went on to greater things.

Programme June 7th 1948. 6pm - 8pm.
Solo. Instruct-Pieces - Cuthbert Harris - M. Kemp
Dreaming-Cradle Song etc. Cuthbert Harris - S. Loveday
Short Pieces - Cuthbert Harris - M. Kemp
Duet. Morning Prayer - Gurlitt - M. Kemp & S. Loveday
Solo. Killarney - B. Sayle.
Memory - C. Harris M. Kemp.
Duets Diligent Pupil - Contest - Gurlitt M. Ager & J. Manning.
Solo. Berenice - Handel C. Edwards.
Memory - Drummer Boy C. Harris etc. J. Evans.
Duet. Longing for Home - Gurlitt - C. Edwards & B. Sayle.
Solo. Dancing - Small Pieces - C. Harris. - J. Evans.
Memory - Soldier's Chorus. - R. Schumann. C. Edwards.
Duet - Hymn of Praise - Gurlitt. M. Ager & J. Rudd.
Solo - Evening Jan Miles M. Sayle.
Solo - Minuet with Variations - Arne. M. Ager.
Memory - The Prelude in C Minor - Rachmaninoff. B. Woods.
Duet - The Butterfly - Gurlitt. - J. Evans & D. Evans.
Solo - Scherzo in F major - Müller J. Manning.
Memory - Fairy Waltz - J.W. Turner. J. Gregory
Duet. Diabelli M & B. Sayle.
Solo - Huntsmen's Chorus. - Weber. J. Rudd.
Memory - Ecossaise - Beethoven. - D. Evans.
Duet. Diabelli - J. Gregory & J. Manning.
Solo. Nocturne Chopin. B. Woods.
Memory - Minuet in D. Haydn M. Ager.

P.T.O.

Duet. Knight Rupert - Gurlitt - J. Evans & J. Rud
Solo - Fantasie in A major Handel D. Evan
Memory - Bourbonnaise. Couperin J. Mannin
Duet. In D Major. Diabelli [illegible] & F.B.
Solo. Toreador - Bizet. J. Rudd.
Memory Minuet in F. - Mozart. B. Say
Duet - Dancing Lesson - Gurlitt. J. Gregory & J. Mannin
Solo - Musical Box. F. Jas. Gossec - M. Ager
Memory. - Ecossaise - Beethoven J. Mann
Duet. Diabelli M. Ager & D. Evan
Solo. Allegro. Beethoven J. Manni
Duet Diabelli J & D Evans.
Solo Prelude in A major Chopin D. Evan
Solo - Waltz from Faust, Gounod. J. Gregor
Solo. Lento - Bartók. J. Grego
Solo - A Little Waltz. Felix Swinstead. C. Edward
Solo. Melodie d'Amour. - Br. Sayle
Memory. God Save the King. J. Rudd.
(Please sing)
An Interval at 7 o'clock

Parties

In spite of it being war-time with food rationing, mothers somehow managed to give their children birthday parties. For weeks beforehand they economised even more than usual on such items as sugar in order to be able to provide a tea to remember. Fish paste sandwiches, jelly and blancmange, biscuits, jam tarts, small cakes and, of course, a birthday cake, with candles if obtainable.

It was not so much the teas that I remember as the games. Party games! Some were the same whoever's party it was, but there were others peculiar to a certain friend.

My earliest memories of parties are pre-war when I was possibly the youngest person there and the games were really for the bigger children. We played Hunt the Thimble, Poor Pussy, The ring on the string, Twilight, Postman's knock, Donkey, Musical chairs and, at 'Auntie' Freda's, something called Trafalgar.

Trafalgar was more of a con-trick than a game and could only be played on a person once. Everyone sat round the room. To those who had never played it was explained that the room was the deck of Captain Horatio Nelson's ship. We all knew what Nelson's ship was called, didn't we? Of course we did! Every English child knew that. The room was to represent the deck of the *Victory*. Various items such as stools and chairs were placed to represent things on deck, lifeboats, guns, buckets and mops. Ropes were held across the room and, in general, lots of obstacles blocked the way from one end of the room to the other. The players must try to remember where all the things were because they would all be sent out of the room, blindfolded and brought one by one to meet Captain Horatio Nelson himself. They must walk the length of the room without tripping over anything. The people in the room would shout instructions to guide them.

Out we went into the hall to await our turn. Blindfold tightly in place we were led in one at a time.

'Watch out!' 'Lift your leg higher!' 'Mind that stool!' 'Bend down lower!'

Carefully the child negotiated all the obstacles and finally got to meet 'Lord Nelson'. A grown-up reminded the child how Lord Nelson had lost his right eye and his right arm.

'Shake hands with Lord Nelson. Here is his arm.'

The child put out its hand to find it was shaking hands with a walking stick in a sleeve. Quite a nasty shock.

'And here is his eye.' And the small hand would be grasped and a finger pushed into a sausage roll.

It was very realistic, gruesome, *horrible*!

The blindfolds were removed and there was a round of applause. The child was then allowed to stay in the room and watch the rest go through it all. Only then did the victims realise they had been conned into believing they had to clamber over things and crawl under them. They saw how all the obstacles had been removed first. It was their turn to call out instructions and to laugh at the horrified faces as fingers were poked into Lord Nelson's missing eye! Ugh!

Murder was *the* game at another friend's. The older ones loved it but it scared the living daylights out of me as they rushed around in the dark and someone screamed, then lay 'dead' on the floor.

But it was my own party one war-time year which I remember for the tea rather than the games, and not so much for the food as for *what happened to it.*

Like other mothers, my mother had been careful with rations so as to be able to make little cakes, jam tarts, jellies and blancmange. The actual birthday cake was a splendid creation made by Mr Elphinstone, a former ship's cook, who lived just round the corner from us in Lambert Road. A few days before the party I had been sent with all the necessary ingredients and now it stood in the centre of the table its pink and yellow layers of sponge covered with white icing and decorated with pink swirls and my name.

My friends had arrived and we were about to start our tea when the new curate came to the door.

'How lovely! A birthday party! Where is the birthday girl?'

'Come in,' Mother said, 'Here she is.'

We were getting a little impatient at this unexpected delay and the curate did not seem in a hurry to leave. Then, no sooner had we taken our first sandwiches, than the air-raid siren went! Quickly we got up, and with our gas masks in our hands, hurried into the shelter.

'Won't you come into the shelter with us, Reverend . . ?' Mother asked.

'No thank you. I'd better stay up here. I've got my Air Raid Warden's hat with me.' And he donned his tin hat. 'I will be all right, thank you.'

Mother and Aunt Nita, who was helping, joined us in the shelter.

'The Reverend . . . is going to brave it out in the house. Seems silly to me.'

'He's got his tin hat.'

'Much good may that do him!'

'No doubt he'll say a prayer or two.'

Mother and Aunt Nita exchanged glances. Then they got us playing 'I spy' and 'I went to the shop and bought . . .' to help pass the time.

Fortunately the warning was not on for long and we cheered as the 'All Clear' sounded.

'Hurray! Now we can get on with the tea!' and we ran up into the house. The curate was just leaving. He raised his tin hat.

'Enjoy your party,' he said, 'I must be away. God bless you!'

We ran into the dining room and stopped dead. Aunt Nita gasped in horror,

'Goodness! Where are all the cakes?' she exclaimed.

Mother was stunned. They looked at each other, then at the disappearing figure of the curate hurrying down the drive.

'They've just gone out of the door!' Mother said flatly.

'No wonder he said he would rather stay up here. The temptation was too much for him again! It's not the first time, is it? May he be forgiven!'

'Huh! But what about the children? That is a shame.' And looking at us Mother apologised, 'I'm sorry my dears, but at least there are some sandwiches and he hasn't touched the *big* cake. Sit down and get started. Let's hope he doesn't come back or there's another siren.'

The curate must have sat at the table and systematically pulled plate after plate of jam tarts and small cakes towards him and eaten almost the lot. We were very disappointed as we had eyed them eagerly. Mother made extra sandwiches but they were not really what we wanted. We had set our hearts and minds and *stomachs* on cakes!

'Goodness! Where are all the cakes?'

Dentists

Of course, parties were something really special for us because we did not have many sweets or fancy cakes. There were no snacks between meals to rot our teeth, but our teeth *did* rot! Perhaps the difficulty in getting toothpaste had something to do with it although, as a chemist's daughter, I can hardly claim that to be the cause. I did not like the taste of peppermint in Pepsodent or Macleans, ('Have you Macleaned your teeth today?') and settled for the Ivory Castles of Gibbs' Dentifrice.

My first real encounter with a dentist was in June 1942 when my father took me to see a Mr Lee. I was given a ride up and down in a big chair, Mr Lee looked into my mouth and - 'whoops' - out came my troublesome tooth. No more pain, no more little plugs of cotton wool soaked in sticky Bunter's Nervine . . . until the next time, of course.

The next time came far too soon but, by then, nice, kind Mr Lee had been called up and was, no doubt, attending to soldiers' teeth somewhere far away. The Bunter's Nervine was in more and more frequent use and nights of broken sleep were becoming commonplace, but dentists were thin on the ground. I began to feel attached to my little holey teeth and the cotton wool plugs, although some of my teeth were beginning to detach themselves from me. They could be wriggled and jiggled and the front ones could rest out flat on my lip. That is, until we were staying with my grandfather at Huntingdon for a few days.

My sister, cousin and myself were happily playing hide-and-seek when we were called to meet 'Uncle John'. None of us had ever heard of him. As far as we knew, *we did not have an Uncle John.* Full of curiosity we ran indoors. Mother and Grandfather were talking to a large man in a grey suit.

'Come and meet Uncle John, Brenda. Give him a big smile'.

I gave a big smile but I was not sure I liked Uncle John. He did not smile, just nodded his head and said, 'Yes'.

'That's all. You can carry on playing now.'

We ran off puzzled but soon forgot Uncle John in our play.

The next day or the day after that, clutching John Mark in one hand and holding Mother's hand with the other, we went with Grandfather's housekeeper for a walk down the High Street to see Uncle John at his house. I was rather surprised to find that there was a shiny brass plate on his front door and began to feel suspicious when the door was opened by a starchy nurse. Fear crept in when she asked me to accompany her to the toilet to 'do a wee-wee.' My protests were ignored and she pulled me towards the lavatory. From there we went into a room where Uncle John was busy. He wore a white coat.

'Come and do a wee-wee.'

'Come and sit in my chair and have a ride.'

There was no escape! Before I had time to start crying, something was shoved between my teeth, a nasty smelling thing was put over my nose, my head felt like bursting and . . . then Mother was coming in to the room - and *she* was holding John Mark - and I thought I had got him with *me*.

'How many?' Mother asked.

'Six,' came the deep voice of Uncle John.

'Hasn't she been a good girl? Six teeth out!'

I was *furious*! Nobody had asked me if I wanted my teeth out! It was no use the grown-ups telling me I would not have any more toothache because, at that moment, I would rather have had my holey teeth and the accompanying toothache than the nasty taste in my mouth. I did not like Uncle John. He was *not* an uncle, after all. It had all been a trick.

I screamed all the way back to Grandfather's house. As we went along the High Street people's heads popped out of shop doorways to discover who was making such a dreadful noise. What had happened?

'She's had some teeth out.' Mother explained to the curious. 'Six'.

Suddenly there was a small hard something in my mouth and my tongue pushed it forwards. My screams reached a new crescendo as I held out number seven! Seven teeth gone! They were *mine* and nobody had asked me. In spite of a visit from the 'tooth fairy' that night it was days before I accepted that the dreadful toothache had gone too . . . but it had, of course.

Fortunately I never met Uncle John again but there were dentists in other places. From then on we paid regular visits to Rigby House in St Giles, Norwich. With sinking stomach we trailed up the hill to disappear down a step and through the black-painted doorway. Once inside we turned right into the waiting room. Black-out curtains pulled across, a dim light and up-right dining chairs like soldiers at attention with backs to the walls. In the centre a dark table strewn with ancient copies of *Punch* and *Picture Post*. Faces looked up silent and miserable to regard every newcomer. When called, the reluctant chosen one crept out and slowly climbed the creaking stairway where the unaccountably cheerful dentist welcomed them into his chair and instructed them to 'open wide'. Lots of questions followed which could not be answered with a mouthful of gadgets and fingers. Fearful eyes watched whirring cords and pulleys, ear-drums felt deafened by the noisy drill and nostrils wrinkled at the smell of burning and cloves. At last the welcome words, 'Rinse and spit' meant the ordeal was finished . . . until the next time.

There always *was* a 'next time' which came too soon for comfort. One time deeply drilled into my memory was when I needed a filling shortly after I had started training to be a nurse. I had not even reached the wards but the large, jovial, white-haired dentist welcomed me in with,

'Come in, *Matron!*'

I sat in the chair.

'We'll soon fill this one. Just a small injection first. This is none of the watered down synthetic stuff they use at your hospital. You'd have to have a syringeful of that whereas you'll only need a tiny drop of this. This is the best. Pure cocaine. Smuggled it in from France.'

The dentist laughed loudly. I thought he was joking but, by the time I had got out of the chair, put on my coat and reached the top of the stairs, I collapsed and was helped into the secretary's room to recover.

I began to think he *had* been telling the truth after all.

Awaydays

We did not have seaside holidays in the 1940s, very few people did. Most of the beaches were forbidden territory and had been mined. Sometimes on a Thursday afternoon or a Sunday we got into Dad's little Standard 9 and set out through the Norfolk countryside. I loved these outings especially when we went blackberrying. Having parked the car in a promising lane we went in search of those delicious fruits, although the largest and juiciest were certain to be out of reach and would be enjoyed by the birds, wasps and flies. My container was never as full as those of the rest of the family when we returned to the car for our picnic, partly because the temptation to eat some was too great but, also, because there was so much else to see - curious insects, birds, wild flowers and, if very lucky, the sight of a bank vole nibbling a toadstool. In the springtime as soon as we passed through the old toll-gate arch on the North Walsham Road we looked to see the lambs in the cherry orchards at Westwick and, later in the year, stopped to buy punnets or baskets of cherries. As summer progressed, swathes of red poppies and the beautiful blue of cornflowers patterned the ripening corn in the neatly-hedged fields. The farmers obviously took great pride in making their hedges stock-proof. Tractors were beginning to replace horses and the stooks of corn were soon to become brick-shaped bales of straw. When herbicides were introduced the cornflowers vanished and the poppies were restricted to the periphery. Electric fencing meant there was no longer need for stock-proof hedging and many of the men who had had those skills were no longer about.

Several times a year we visited a great-aunt at Mundesley-on-sea where she kept a small guest-house. The railway line ran across the bottom of her garden so we were told to keep clear of that and, as our great-aunt had to dig a trench, also at the end of the garden, in which to empty the lavatory bucket every day, we did! Inside her house several framed illuminated Biblical texts hung on the walls. In the dining room 'Choose you this day whom ye will serve.' (Joshua. Ch.24. v.15) would have roused doubts in the minds of guests . . . . especially during rationing!

Much of our summer holidays from school was spent at home in the garden. On an old ground-sheet and blanket spread on the grass in the shade of the apple trees we stretched out, Margaret possibly reading aloud from

Little Women whilst I watched the clouds drift across the blue sky, fascinated by their ever-changing shapes. Next door Mr P. was cutting the grass, the rhythmic Rrrrr --- thrrrrr of the push-and-pull Qualcast mower dreamily belying the amount of effort needed. Sometimes we took the wind-up 'His Master's Voice' gramophone and records to amuse us, winding the handle, carefully placing the needle on to the record to listen to George Formby 'All by yourself in the Moonlight' and Flotsam and Jetsom singing 'Maud Marie' and 'Little Joan', one voice reaching incredible depths, especially when the speed no longer reached 78 rpm because the handle needed re-winding. We giggled as we re-wound the handle and the voices rose to the proper pitch. Time and again we listened to Ernest Luff singing 'O for the Wings of a Dove' and there were many others including 'Me and Jane in a Plane' and 'Once in love with Amy' and the 'Micky, Tricky Mouse Foxtrot', in fact, all the latest from Mother and Dad's courting days. It was not until after the war that we would be able to buy new records and I remember putting Eddie Calvert's 'O my Papa' and 'Cherry Pink' on the turntable time after time. Long-play records were years in to the future and it was not until my 21st birthday that I became the proud owner of my first one, which was Rawicz and Landauer playing at two pianos. Next came Gustav Holst and The Planets Suite, chosen after sitting and listening to it in a booth at Willmott's store. Many happy hours were spent in booths of record shops listening and deciding which one to buy, but these could not be played on the old HMV gramophone and Dad bought one of the new Regentone Radiograms which was a great improvement.

When he managed to get a locum pharmacist for the shop Dad took us to Huntingdon, the 80-mile journey taking about three hours. When we went there one Christmas-time it was a freezing cold journey because, of course, there was no heating in the car but, just before we left home, our kind neighbour had given us large roasting-hot potatoes to hold to keep us warm en route. It was a very quiet road as we meandered through all the small towns. At one point we looked out for Kett's Oak and there was another tree, self-sown, growing alone on the heath and standing tall at the edge of the road. It could be seen for seven miles and was a favourite land-mark for us. Another thing I remember is seeing flowers on the grass by a cross-roads and we were told they were on a gypsy's grave.

All through the war Dad and his father took it in turns to telephone each other just after closing time on Saturday nights. Sometimes we walked down to the shop and were also able to talk to Grandfather. We did not have a telephone at home. At one time businesses which had telephones were listed in the local newspaper. The shop telephone was tall and black with the receiver resting in a clip at the side. It was always exciting to be the one to get the operator and ask for Huntingdon 187 and then listen as the call went along the line, Wymondham, Thetford, Newmarket, Cambridge, Huntingdon and when Grandfather answered, make him guess who was calling!

It was better still to go to Huntingdon to stay. Even after Nanny Sayle's death it was always a magical place for us. Grandfather liked to take us to church with him on a Sunday morning. Having wound the grandfather clock, checked his pocket watch, collected his hat and walking-stick from the hall he strode out proudly with us, his three grand-daughters, (our cousin Betty, Margaret and myself,) and Mother and Dad to walk the short distance along the High Street to All Saints' Church. There were always noisy rooks nesting in the tall trees by the church railings and they could be heard above the peal of bells. Inside the church Dad pointed out various items of interest. He had been a chorister there.

It was exciting to be so close to all the shops and once the war was over and books started to appear on the shelves we made a bee-line for W.H.Smith's. Carefully saved pocket-money was handed over for the latest Enid Blyton or an Observer's Book.

We took Grandfather's dog for walks over the commons; from the bridge over the main railway line we watched smelly smoky steam trains noisily come and go and we 'helped' in Grandfather's shop. It was a much bigger shop than Dad's although Grandfather did not dispense medicines. Old drug jars filled the top shelves and all the drawers bore latin names in gold-leaf. In one drawer we found heavy dental forceps - and we were told of the time when Grandfather had agreed to a friend's request to draw a tooth! We gathered that the patient took a large measure of whisky before the ordeal and they both finished the bottle afterwards! Our delight was when we were allowed to make the hand-cream which was much in demand. On one small table assorted cakes of unwrapped soap were displayed and on another a large selection of Heath & Heather herbs. The memory of that table is roused every time I open a packet of spices or curry powder.

One Easter my holiday was almost ruined by an accident in the stable yard. Mother was recuperating after an operation to remove her appendix. In the morning Grandfather's housekeeper had taken us by train to visit her brother and his wife at Offord and, on our return, we played hide-and-seek whilst she prepared supper. Betty and I had hidden in the stable loft where Margaret soon discovered us. As we made our way down the steps I turned to speak to one of them, put my hand out to the rail, missed it and plummeted down to the cobbled yard! I can still see those cobbles coming to meet me. My screams brought the grown-ups in to the yard and Grandfather's housekeeper, 'Auntie Dot', picked me up and carried me in to the kitchen. Dr Connan was called, came immediately, decided against stitching and strapped my chin together with Elastoplast. A few days later I was as right as rain but we had strict instructions not to venture up to the loft again.

In any case the stable yard had been taken over by the army. Places where we had played were labelled 'Officers mess' or 'Out of Bounds' and army equipment was all around. After the war, when the soldiers had gone, a dairy rented the space and installed equipment for pasteurising the milk. The machine stood in a large stable, open to the air and, as we skipped in the yard, we watched the milk trickling over the screen as it was heated to a certain temperature then rapidly cooled but, obviously, they were less than hygienic conditions. It was not long before the yard was used merely for transferring bottled milk to delivery vans and we were woken early from our sleep by an incredibly noisy clatter.

The stable yard

Peace

In September 1943 Granny and Grandfather moved into a home of their own and we no longer had to sleep down the 'dug-out' every night. In spite of dampness and the cramped conditions there had been some lighter moments such as the evening when a cat had walked across my pillow. I was thrilled because I loved animals and tried to keep it hidden, but when Mother came to bed she heard it purring so - outside it went! And outside in the pitch-blackness a shemozzle took place one night when two men were cycling past, one of them with a box full of rabbits strapped on his carrier. Evidently, in the darkness, the men collided, the box fell off and the rabbits escaped! Mother was doubled up with laughter listening to their language as they desperately tried to catch the animals. Usually the excitement amounted to no more than attempting to beat the record for swatting gnats, attracted to the hurricane lamp.

The war dominated our lives in many ways, of course. We slept in the dug-out most of the time. In 1942 Miss Bidewell had to close her school for a few weeks whilst bomb damage was repaired - not that I minded because I still preferred home to school. Margaret had left Ebenezer House and was enjoying being at the Notre Dame High School. If *that* school had still been a boarding school there is no doubt she would have wanted to be a boarder. Nothing would keep her away unnecessarily.

However, one very chilly morning, Mother spotted something which meant we would both have to stay away from school for a few weeks. My clothes were warming on the big guard and I was dressing in front of the kitchen fire as the bedroom temperature was near freezing. Suddenly Mother noticed some spots on my chest and back. Chicken pox! At least we did not have to go to the Isolation Hospital for that. I lived in fear of having to be taken off in the dreaded 'fever van', an old ambulance, which I had noticed on occasion creeping slowly down the road. We had had measles and whooping cough. One of my earliest memories is of sitting on Mother's lap in a darkened room where a night light burned in a lamp which gave off coal-tar fumes, whilst I coughed and whooped and gagged. We were immunised against diphtheria and I did not catch mumps. But chicken-pox meant three weeks away from school and was worth all the itching and scratching. We stayed in bed to begin with and enjoyed being fussed over by Mother who brought us hot-water-bottles and drinks and little meals on trays. It was not long before we were feeling better.

From our garden we watched formations of Lancaster bombers heading for the coast and Germany. We counted them when they returned and were saddened to realise some were missing. There were times when barrage balloons broke away from their moorings and drifted dangerously with the wind. But, eventually, the war began to turn in our favour and when I wished fervently for peace as I stirred the Christmas pudding in 1944, there was a chance that wish might become reality.

In the first week of May 1945 Germany surrendered. We listened to King George VI and to Winston Churchill on the wireless. We went into Norwich to see the Victory Parade and to special Church services. There was no more need for Air-raid shelters or black-out. We were taken to the Pictures and the Theatre Royal and the Hippodrome, now without any worries about sirens. In fact, throughout the war we had been to Pantomimes and other suitable performances. In June Mother's diary records that we had our first ride in Dad's car *for three years*. Life was beginning to return to how it should be.

But the war with Japan was not over until the August and then only after the atomic bombs had been dropped. It was at night on 14th August 1945 that news of the Japanese surrender came through and we were on holiday at Huntingdon. I shall always remember hearing the crowd thronging through the High Street, looking down from our bedroom windows on to the torch-light procession wending its way from the north of the town to the market square.

The torch-light procession

New things

Opposite Grandfather's shop was a draper's from where, every time we stayed at Huntingdon, new ribbons were bought for my pigtails. Inside the shop Flo and Gus reigned over umpteen drawers full of such things as buttons, bindings, belts, bobbins and bows and, although they grumbled about the difficulty of getting stock, to me even in war-time the shop seemed brimming over with every sort of trimming imaginable. As war ended, a new material was entering our lives - plastic! Instead of pretty silky ribbons I was given long strips of pink and purple plastic. The purple plastic ribbons were for school use of course. I did not like the smell of them - it reminded me of gas, but some children loved the smell and even the *taste* of plastic. Besides the flat ribbon strips we could buy different coloured plastic like string with which we transformed our hair-grips into slides. The plastic ribbons were a novelty but did not last long as they tore easily.

Wool, not plastic, was what I was trying to use as I attempted to knit. I had only just learned to do purl as well as knit and my work was very tight on the needles. It was not easy. At the same time Mother was making fire-lighters from old newspapers. I watched her roll the large sheets of paper, flatten the roll then, starting at the centre, flick one side over the other alternately before tucking in the end to keep it firm. I had seen her do that many times before. How neat they were! She put them in the fireplace and placed a few sticks of kindling on top but paused before adding the coals.

'Don't you think it is time you finished those bootees?' she asked, smiling at me.

The bootees in question were the first proper knitting I had ever attempted. I was not good at knitting but a friend of Mother's had a daughter who had just had a baby and these bootees were to have been a present for that baby. The baby had already arrived and was growing fast. We spoke about the baby then Mother said,

'Perhaps I'll keep the bootees.'

'No! No, they are for *Barbara's* baby.'

'They will be too small for her. I think I will keep them in case I have a baby myself.' Mother was watching me carefully. What was she saying?

That was the first inkling I had that I would be having a new baby sister - or brother. It took time to sink in. Every Christmas I wrote a letter to Father Christmas and always my list of wants started with 'a baby brother' or 'a dog'. The nearest I had got to either was when Dad bought some day-old chicks for me and I had been delighted.

One lunch-time when walking along Denmark Road towards Sprowston Road from Miss Bidewell's I noticed Dad standing at his shop entrance. He waved to me to cross the road. It seemed dark and cool inside the shop and he took me into his back room where there was a cardboard box with holes in it and from the box came little cheeps and scratchings. We peeped inside. Four day-old chicks!

'Do you think you can manage to take them home on the 'bus?' Dad asked.

I nodded excitedly.

'Your Mother will know what to do with them. Mind how you go.'

I crossed the road again and went to wait at the 'bus stop. The 'bus was not long in coming and I sat just inside carefully holding the box upright. The chicks started chirping again and all the other passengers turned to look.

'Oh! She's got some chickens!' they smiled at each other and at me. I glowed with happiness.

The short journey of two stops was soon over. Carefully I climbed down the step of the 'bus when it stopped outside The Brickmakers' Arms. As usual, two or three of the 'regulars' sat in the shade on the roots of the magnificent copper beech tree, pints of best Bullard's Norwich ale leaving creamy froth on their moustaches as they lowered their glasses. They always had something to say,

'Lovely day, Missy!' as I hurried past in the hot sunshine, panama hat held in place by elastic. Or, when the hot weather was boiling up towards a storm,

'Mearke you haste, Missy! Them ther' be tempest clouds!'

'Moind how yer goo!'

And on this occasion, 'W'ot 'a yew got some chicks in ther'?'

I nodded, blushed as usual, and carried on walking primly past them, then crossed Sprowston Road and walked round by the post office into Mousehold Lane. It seemed an extra long walk as I held the box in front of me and looked neither to right nor left. After the group of houses I crossed the 'desert' as we called the sandy car-park by The Duke of Norfolk which provided Steward & Patterson's ale, from another Norwich brewer, for its customers. At the back of the car park the greyhound race-track lay silent behind the wooden fencing during the day, but was filled with exciting noise twice a week now the war was over. Opposite, in the garden of the house on the corner of Alford Grove, behind the wrought iron gate and the high wall topped with broken glass, the two Miss Gillings were tending their impeccable garden and further along Mrs H. was standing in her driveway facing the long privet hedge. I knew that behind the hedge on the opposite side of Blackwell Avenue, Mrs T. would also be standing in her driveway, facing *her* hedge. At one time I had been scared of the 'talking hedges' but not now, although as soon as I was seen by Mrs H. I knew word would pass through the hedges that I had some chicks. It was unnerving to think the two ladies could see without being seen. They missed nothing.

At home Mother was ready and waiting for the four chicks. I watched them, fascinated, wondering if they would lay eggs for us when they grew up. One of them died after a few days, the other three were cockerels and were destined to become dinners - but I did not know that then. Hours were spent watching them, seeing their fluff change to feathers and digging the ground so they could find worms.

They were the only living things I had had, but now my wish for a baby brother or sister was likely to become true and that was much more exciting.

The finished bootees were put with all the other baby things in the cot, ready and waiting. Clothing coupons were still needed, so Mother made nightdresses from her aunt's Victorian petticoats. I was very unsure about where the baby was or how it would be born but I knew we were all looking forward to its arrival, boy or girl.

Then, one night, just after we had gone to sleep, Dad crept in to our bedroom to tell us that he was taking Mother to the Nursing Home. Soon after he came back, our little sister was born. Of course we wanted to know what she looked like, but children were not allowed in to the Nursing Home and we had to be patient for a whole fortnight, then, one afternoon, I went with Dad to fetch Mother and the baby. The nurse came down the stairs and placed a bundle of white shawls into my arms and in the shawls I could just see a tiny face, eyes tight shut fast asleep, and a tuft of very fair hair. She was lovely!

Soon after we got back to our house Margaret arrived home from school. The baby was still asleep and we waited impatiently for her to open her eyes. Then, enraptured, we heard her cry for the first time.

A few months later, wearing the family christening gown, hand sewn by a great-great-aunt, she was christened, Diane Mary, at St Cuthbert's Church.

There was much for us to learn, helping Mother in all sorts of ways, going for walks pushing the pram, pegging out the washing, ironing or shopping. Quite often I went with Margaret to do the shopping in Magdalen Street, one of the narrow medieval streets stretching from the old city walls into the centre of Norwich. It was a very busy shopping area, especially on Fridays when the factory workers from nearby shoe factories swarmed into the street after getting their pay packets. We did our shopping earlier in the day, perhaps taking a doll to be repaired at The Dolls' Hospital, a fascinating old shop once full of glass eyes, teddy-bears, dolls and dolls' clothes but, in war-time, the stock was depleted. Close by was the large store of Frank Price where Mother bought our vests, underwear and pyjamas (in June 1943 a pair of pyjamas accounted for six clothing coupons). Further along the street was Woolworth's, 'the 3d. and 6d. store' and we usually made our way around its counters, our footsteps sounding loud on the wooden floorboards - but not as loud as in the 'cheaper' Peacock's bazaar on the other side of the road, which never seemed to have any customers, and where the very young assistants stood behind the continuous counters watching our self-conscious progress, no doubt longing for someone to make a purchase! Sometimes Mother asked us to go to Loose's, a high class shop well known for quality china and glass but, during the war, customers were lucky if they could buy even odd white earthenware mugs, such was the scarcity of goods. Loose's sold hardware, too, and all Mother was likely to ask us to look for were asbestos mats - small metal-edged discs of asbestos to put under saucepans during cooking, to prevent burning.

Usually our shopping instructions were to get the grocery rations. We were registered at Whiting's on Sprowston Road for meat and eggs (and there were times when a family of four could only get four eggs for the week, although tinned 'powdered egg' was sometimes available.) For some of our groceries we were registered with the Maypole in Magdalen Street. There were several grocery shops within a few yards of each other, including the Home and Colonial, Lipton's and the International. Shopping had to be done every week and every week it took a long time and a lot of patience. The counters were all round the shop and sections of them were for specific items. There was a cheese counter, a bacon counter, counters for butter, margarine, lard, sugar and biscuits and at every counter there was a queue! Customers moved from one queue to the next, the manager of the shop attempting to keep everything under control. We groaned when Mother asked us to go to the Maypole but, with a small baby, she needed our help.

Also in Magdalen Street was the branch of Barclays Bank where Dad had his business account. Sometimes we were instructed to go in there and ask for the manager, give him a written note and get whatever was required. It was all very personal.

Another errand connected with Dad's shop was to take an order in to the wholesale chemists, Smith & Sons, also in Magdalen Street. How important it felt to climb up the steps and enter the front door of the impressive Georgian building even if it was only to hand a piece of paper to a girl behind a desk.

Then we waited outside The Dolls' Hospital for the 'bus to take us home. Whenever I waited there I thought about a young boy who Mother

We waited outside The Dolls' Hospital for the 'bus to take us home.

and I had once seen being dragged along the pavement on the opposite side of the street. It was a burning hot day and, as usual, there was no traffic about apart from an ancient bicycle being propelled along by an old man singing something about 'no-where to go in the *snow*'. The *snow*! We were melting in the heat! Perhaps it was the heat which had got to the woman and the young boy as they went past Spurgeon's the Pork Butcher's. Inside the shop the butcher was making sausages. The boy was screaming his head off. His mother shrieked above his screaming,

'If you don't b . . . well shut up I'll ask that butcher to put you in his machine and turn *you* into sausages!'

The boy screamed even louder. The silent street flooded with his terror.

'Dreadful woman!' said Mother in disgust. 'Fancy telling the poor little chap *that*!'

Mother nearly always took the child's side.

Then, at long last, the number 91 'bus came in to sight and we started on our journey home. Possibly I was uncommonly quiet as we rattled towards Sprowston, pondering the fate of the screaming boy. I was extremely thankful that Mother was *my mother*.

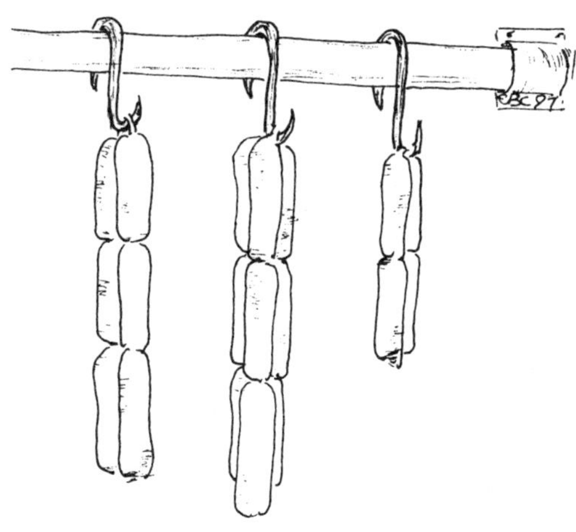

Preparatory School

Miss Bidewell was thinking of retiring and Ebenezer House School would close after more than fifty years. Such a school would never exist again. It had been a remnant of the Victorian era where the children had been given individual attention and developed at their own pace. Here, in a small group, they learned to show respect for their elders, understanding for those less able than themselves, consideration for everybody and a healthy respect for their own and other people's property. Whilst they would lack experience on a playing field, their classroom abilities were equal, if not superior, to those of children from the State schools. Miss Bidewell had plenty of patience and we were well versed in the 'three R's'.

When I was nine years old the decision was taken that I should sit the entrance examination for the preparatory section of the Notre Dame High School. Thus it was that on Saturday morning, 7th December 1946, Margaret took me with her to the school. Margaret often went to the school on Saturday mornings for netball practice or tennis, or for elocution.

Getting off the 'bus at Tombland meant there was quite a walk up to the school. We went across the Cattle Market, where the market was already in full swing. I had not seen it like that before and was fascinated by all the animals, the farmers and the men wearing caps, smoking pipes and prodding the sheep and cattle with their sticks. Perhaps it was as well that we did not have time to stop because it *was*, as Mother had said, a *horrible* place in some ways and she felt sorry for the animals. She hated seeing any animal trapped in a cage. I realised what she meant when I caught sight of a calf trying to get to its mother's over-flowing udder but was in a separate pen with no hope of reaching the cow. Their cries and moos were pitiful. There was a lot of moo-ing and baa-ing in the stalls and most of the animals looked bewildered. We hurried through, past the rabbits and chickens. I had difficulty keeping up with Margaret, but eventually we reached Surrey Street. My mind had been so busy thinking about the Cattle Market that I had almost forgotten the reason I was there - and my future depended on it!

Three places were being offered at the Preparatory School and there were three of us sitting the examinations. The other two girls were sisters, one of them slightly older than myself and the other about a year younger. We were taken into a classroom, papers put before us and a nun supervised as we tackled questions on arithmetic and vocabulary and wrote a short essay. When it was over Margaret shepherded me home. I did not have long to wait for the result because two days later a note came to say I would be placed in Prep.6. As this was the top class in the prep. school and there were only two terms left of the school year it meant I would not be there for long. In one way putting me into the top class, where most of the children were older than I, was a mistake because when the time came for me to take the school leaving certificate I was too young. With two other girls who had been in that Prep. 6, because our birthdays were after the first of September, I could not sit the examinations with the rest of our year and had to wait until the following July.

On the first morning of my first term Margaret accompanied me up to the Prep. school and left me with a teacher. I was shown the cloakrooms and one of the girls was detailed to look after me. We went into our classroom where I was to share a double desk with another girl immediately in front of the teacher's desk. Our form-mistress was a tall, somewhat severe looking nun, Sister Thérèse. Before lessons started there was assembly where all the classes stood in their ranks before the headmistress. The headmistress, Sister Augustine, was a tiny little woman smaller than many of the pupils, and the eldest of them was only eleven years old. After prayers and a hymn, Sister Augustine gave out any notices or instructions before we returned to our classrooms. More than once I was the reluctant centre of attention as she admonished me because I was not yet wearing the school uniform. Instead of a tunic of marine blue (which I think was the correct name for that particular shade of green), a cream blouse and rust tie, my grey skirt, white blouse and fair-isle cardigan stood out. I was very conscious of being different, but Mother had been unable to obtain a uniform for me. Green's, the school outfitters, was the only store from which they could be obtained. Uniforms were made to order and clothing coupons were necessary. It all took an age and, possibly, by the time it arrived I would be in the High School where a different pattern of tunic was required. In any case, summer dresses would be in order after Whitsun. Eventually Mother managed to get a second-hand outfit for me and Sister Augustine was satisfied.

First days at a new school can never be easy. Certainly my first day at Notre Dame Preparatory School was something of a shock to me. For one thing there were so many children, about 200 of them, rushing about in the play area. I was absolutely scared they would knock me over and stood near to the teacher on playground duty. Inside the classroom again all was strange. We did some writing and Sister Thérèse asked to see mine. I took it to her and it was immediately obvious that she was *not* pleased. She looked coldly at me through her tortoiseshell-rimmed round spectacles and twitched her top lip.

'*Nobody* taught you to write like this!' she declared. 'It will not do!'

All the carefully practised up-strokes and down-strokes and the twirls of copper-plate hand-writing which Miss Bidewell had tried to teach us would not do for the Notre Dame. That evening, almost in tears, I had to practise making large block capital 'A's instead of the pretty copperplate one. The thing which upset me most was not having to alter my writing but the fact that Sister Thérèse would not accept that that was how I had been taught. She did not believe I was telling the truth and, as I was, that hurt.

One of my favourite lessons was art and it was in my first art lesson, sitting next to a very kind girl, the tallest in the class, that I began to feel I belonged. We had our art lessons in the dining room which was, in effect, part of the assembly hall, a partition dividing it into two. For the first time ever I was given a large sheet of paper to work on. In war-time at Miss Bidewell's a page from a drawing book was divided into small areas about three inches by four inches and we had to produce a picture in that. Small wonder that my first attempts at making a poster depicting 'winter sports' were ridiculed by the teacher because all the figures were minuscule.

At least by the time I started at Notre Dame the War had ended. A friend recalls how petrified she had been as a little child of five, when all was talk of Hitler and the Blitz, being taken to school past bombed sites through a city where buildings disappeared overnight. One never knew what would be next. Then, at school, there was much teaching of Catechism and learning about Sin and Death, Eternity, Heaven, and Hell, and, if one was not baptised one could not enter Heaven. *Not enter Heaven!* In panic she rushed home to discover if she was baptised. Yes, as a member of the *Congregational* church she was - but what about her Mother? Was she? Her Mother *did not know*!! Horror of horrors!! To go to Heaven, or Hell, or even Limbo without her Mother was unthinkable and she nearly had a nervous breakdown. Small children can become confused by too much doctrine. Some use it to their advantage! The young daughter of a friend of my Mother became impossibly naughty after starting at the Notre Dame

Preparatory School and her Mother was near despair. They were not Roman Catholics so, until then, the little girl did not know the 'Hail Mary'. She thought that she could do anything she wanted to and, provided she said a Hail Mary after her misdeeds, she would be forgiven. With that comforting thought she proceeded to be as naughty as possible! An aunt (obviously not a Catholic) of one little girl heard her recite the Hail Mary and was disgusted to hear the words, 'Blessed is the *fruit of thy womb*, Jesus'. 'What did you say, child?' she demanded. 'Wherever did you learn such words? Do you know what they mean?' Of course the child did not know what they meant. Who, in those days, would explain the word 'womb' to someone so young? Such things were never spoken in polite society and certainly not in front of the children.

Being right in the convent, religion was very evident. There was an air of reverence everywhere. Occasionally we were taken to the Convent Chapel. Beeswax candles and many prayers spoken softly in the gentle light produced a feeling of hushed awe.

In the playground I was still afraid of the children dashing about playing tag or skipping. I had never seen children playing tag because there had been no room for such a game at Ebenezer House. Some of the children could skip for hours discovering their chances of getting married, whether they would wear silk, satin, muslin or rags and ride in a coach, carriage, wheelbarrow or muck cart! (No mention of wedding *cars* in this ancient skipping rhyme!) With a girl either end of a long rope, as many as possible skipped together 'All in together, girls. Never mind the weather, girls. Fetch a coat and put it on. Tell your Mother you won't be long.' Some did keep going for a long while but not me, I was too fearful of falling over.

One way of avoiding the playground was to help clear away the dinner things. School dinners were delivered to the school in large metal containers. Girls from the High School came to serve them to us. Margaret and her friends in the Form III of the High School were servers for a time. I did not really like the food which was quite often greasy stew, or mince and slimy potato, semolina or, worse still, tapioca 'frogs' spawn' and jam. When the left-overs were cold there was a thick layer of fat covering them. Once I pulled out the ladle covered in this congealed mess and started to chase one of my sister's friends with it but, just at that moment, a door opened and one of the nuns had a very near miss! So did I! Quickly disappearing into the depths of the dark kitchen I slid the ladle into the sink and stood still, heart pounding, whilst the nun delivered a little lecture on 'unacceptable behaviour'.

Being in the Prep. school did not give us automatic right of entry into the High School. We all had to sit the entrance examination. Other entrants would come from the various schools throughout the city and, because it was a Roman Catholic School, throughout the county of Norfolk too. Some of them would gain entrance by passing the 11+ scholarship.

The Sisters of Notre Dame had been invited to come to Norwich in 1864 and first established a boarding school. In 1896, day pupils were admitted. In 1924 an up-to-date modern school had been erected and this was the building where we hoped to go. According to an *Illustrated Souvenir of the Convent of Notre Dame in Norwich* the Order of the Sisters of Notre Dame aimed to train the moral character of girls, fostering the virtues of Truth, Gentleness, Charity and a sense of honour. They hoped to educate 'in the highest sense of the word - to send great souls into the world, girls who are precious to their surroundings and precious to themselves . . . (to) build a character full of hope and courage, and the spirit of perseverance. Such become people of worth who can be trusted with responsibility, and this is no mean thing in life.'

Unaware of these high ideals we answered the questions on the entrance examination as best we could and waited somewhat anxiously to learn the outcome.

Eventually a small scrap of green paper, somewhat resembling a raffle ticket, was sent to my parents announcing that I had been accepted for the Notre Dame High School and would be placed in Form 1. Would it be a lucky ticket? Undoubtedly on the whole it was, but I never *enjoyed* school as much as my sisters did.

The form assigned is provisional, and may be altered before theopening of term.

NOTRE DAME HIGH SCHOOL, NORWICH

The Headmistress is pleased to inform you that
Brenda Sayle
has been accepted as a pupil of the Notre Dame High School. She will be placed in I and her first day of attendance will be Sept.16th!47 Kindly confirm in writing your acceptance of this vacancy for your child by filling in the enclosed Form and returning it to the Headmistress immediately.

NOTE. Admission to the Preparatory Department or to the Transition Class does not necessarily imply subsequent admission to the Secondary Department. Admission to the Secondary Department is granted to those pupils only who have attained a sufficiently high standard of work, and who show aptitude for a Grammar School course. A satisfactory record of conduct and observance of School Regulations is also obligatory.

...resembling a raffle ticket...

Notre Dame High School

Notre Dame High School catered for between 500 and 600 pupils. They were divided into three streams for each of the five years and then there was a lower sixth form and an upper sixth form. Children were selected for the different streams according to their aptitudes. Those showing more academic promise were placed in Form 1 (or, correctly named, Form 1 *Latin*), next came the 'alpha' stream and those of a more practical nature in the 'A' stream. Throughout their schooling pupils could be moved into a different stream if it was considered advisable and beneficial to the pupil.

However, once in a Form, that Form became like a family. We belonged to each other and shared in each other's achievements - and disgraces. This belonging, this being a single unit, was cemented by the fact that we stayed within our classroom for most lessons and the teachers came to us. The exceptions to this were art, needlework, science and physical training (P.T. as it was called before becoming P.E., physical education). Every form had its own Form Mistress responsible for the class and who provided the Religious Instruction and, possibly, her particular subject, but most of the lessons were given by specialist teachers travelling from classroom to classroom.

The classrooms were bright and airy. The lower part of the wall tiled with blue/green tiles, a colour similar to our uniform tunics. The upper part was cream. Large windows overlooked the convent gardens where the apple trees bordered the path between school and convent and where the nuns often took their communal walk. There were possibly thirty five desks in neat rows of seven by five. Thirty-five was the usual number of pupils per class. They were very good desks, solid and square, the lid lifting to reveal an inner well for textbooks and a shelf for exercise books. There was an ink-well, the ink being supplied by the school - 'Stephen's scholastic blue-black ink', a type reconstituted, I believe, from a powder and which was inclined to ruin our fountain pens. We were pleased when we were able to buy, and be allowed to have, our own bottles of ink, Stephen's or Quink. Large blackboards were fixed to the wall. There was a pulpit-like desk for the teacher in which the seat and desk were in one unit. This was all right for the taller mistresses but cannot have suited the shorter women. In fact, I have been told about the gymnastic efforts one very tiny nun used to make in order to be seated before her class. Her subject - Spelling, her name - Sister Eustelle. That name, not surprisingly, came in for corruption! Evidently, Sister Eustelle would enter the classroom,

'Good Morning!' she greeted her class. 'Now let me hear the "Good"!' And the class would chorus 'GOOD Morning, Sister Euspell,' or whatever variant was their choice for the day, and giggle at their inventiveness. And, whilst they were bowing and greeting the little nun, she would be grasping hold of the desk and executing a backward leap so she might sit upon the too-high seat. Needless to say, the class watched incredulously. Unfortunately I never witnessed this feat as she had left before my time.

Not all the nuns were teachers and not all the teachers were nuns. The majority were, of course, Roman Catholics. Of the pupils possibly less than 10% were RCs. Religion played a large part in our school lives. We had a lesson of Religious Instruction every day and we said the 'Hail Mary' between lessons and the Angelus was recited at lunchtime. Morning assembly was held daily in the panelled Assembly Hall.

Every class formed into a rank in the front of its classroom; smallest at the front behind the form prefect, then in ascending height to the back.

Our turn arrived. Then it was,

'No talking!' and, with Westminster Hymnals in our hands, we proceeded in orderly fashion, to the Assembly Hall, bowing low as we passed any teachers. We were always bowing! Every time we passed a teacher or one of the several statues on the corridors we bowed and, if a teacher had cause to visit when a class was in progress, we all stood up, bowed, and remained standing quietly whilst that teacher was in the room. Some of us astounded our parents by bowing automatically whenever we passed them at home. Our way to the Assembly Hall was 'policed' by Sixth Form Prefects placed at the bottom and top of the stairways keenly ensuring we did keep quiet and behave. They could give '*Black Marks* for our *House*' if we whispered or pushed and, of course, we did not want that disgrace but prefects seemed to have extra acute hearing sometimes! In the Assembly Hall we stood in silent ranks the length of the hall. On the stage, the Head Girl watched over us until the Headmistress took the platform. It was a lofty hall, half panelled, and on one wall hung the Honours Board bearing in gold letters the names of girls who had achieved university degrees. In those days not many girls were admitted to universities but, gradually, numbers increased. My sisters' names would be among them.

Bowing low as we passed a teacher

When we were all assembled - and *totally* quiet - the Headmistress entered. During my early years at Notre Dame High School this was Sister St James, 'Jimmy' amongst ourselves. Pale, small, and wearing round spectacles, she somehow commanded respect. When she retired her place was taken by a much younger woman, Sister Marie. Tall and dignified we always held her in awe. I do not recall us ever giving her a nickname. From the beginning she stirred us from complacency. Not long after her arrival, during morning assembly one day she asked if any of us could name the school flower. School flower? We did not know there was such a thing. But, Sister Marie informed us, we passed it every time we entered a classroom because on the door the number of the Form was written in the centre of - a marigold! 'Mary's Gold'! How unobservant we all were!

The Assembly Hall was also where we had our singing lessons with Miss Rena Cocks, a highly skilled musician and a concert pianist who would have enjoyed the glamour of the international stage but for the travel restrictions caused by the war. She had to be content with us and we were lucky to have her. She was the sole music teacher and taught throughout the school. Miss Cocks had the distinction of being the only teacher to own a car, a small black vehicle which she parked behind the school and which caused us to flatten ourselves against the school wall at the end of the day to let it squeeze past. Most teachers walked or cycled; a few came by train or 'bus.

On our first day in year one we were gathered together in the dining room and sorted into 'houses'. The school had three houses: Walsingham, Stafford and Townley. At one time there had been a fourth: Lourdes. Because Margaret was already in Walsingham I was put into Walsingham, too. Walsingham, we thought, was the best. Stafford and Townley members felt the same about their houses, of course. We wore small badges declaring our allegiance and, after Whitsun, when we wore our summer uniform dresses our house was obvious because the flowery dresses with white collars and cuffs, although the same pattern, had the predominant colour of the house: Blue for Walsingham, Yellow for Stafford or Green for Townley. As it was so soon after the war, clothing coupons were still needed. Then there was the lengthy business of being measured for them at Green's and waiting for them to arrive. When they did we were none too pleased that the waist dipped a lot below the belt - presumably we were expected to have huge bosoms to fill the bodice - but, of course, we did not!

Uniform was strictly enforced. During the summer term we had to wear the dresses just described, short white ankle socks (although, one year, there was a scare that we were to have long white stockings! Horrors! The rumour went that the stockings had already arrived at Green's and we really began to believe we were doomed to be the laughing stock of the City of Norwich.). Panama hats, with elastic under the chin, a Notre Dame-green band and the school badge were to be worn. Unfortunately, the vagaries of English weather meant that a sunny morning suitable for the panama might turn to rain - and we must NEVER be seen without our hat - and the panama became a sunken mess forever thereafter out of shape. We had school blazers in 'our' green with pocket badge worked in rust. However hot the weather when school reopened in September after the 8-week long summer holidays, we had to wear our winter uniforms - a green (marine blue) tunic, a cream blouse (and *nothing* must be worn *over* it although extra warmth could be provided by having a jumper, preferably white, *under* it but, when I was in the fifth year, Notre Dame-green cardigans were a welcome introduction), a rust tie, brown knee-socks, held up by garters, and brown lace leather shoes for outdoor wear, brown bar-shoes for indoors. In our third year we went in to stockings and discovered the problems of keeping the seams straight, mending ladders and wearing suspender belts (not easily obtained). We had green (marine blue) gaberdine raincoats, which were not proof against anything more than a light shower, and felt hats to match which soon lost their shape, resulting in girls putting in tucks and more tucks until the hat resembled a beret. When, rather than if, seen by a teacher a summons to the Headmistress was inevitable. Once plastics were introduced there were plastic rain-hoods in rust colour but they tore easily. Brown leather kid gloves had to be worn with winter uniform, white gloves in summer. We wore white tennis shoes for P.T. and, as wartime restrictions eased, sportswear was introduced - green shorts and white aertex blouses; I believe my year was the first to benefit from these. Until then, apart from changing shoes, P.T.was done in full uniform of blouse and tunic. After a strenuous session in the gymnasium the atmosphere must have been far from pleasant in the classroom as there were no shower facilities.

There was much to take in on our first morning. Those of us who had been in the prep school were at an advantage; at least we knew someone. However there was another group of friends from a school just outside the City of Norwich who, having passed the scholarship had elected to come to the Notre Dame so, even if everything was strange to them, they did have friends already. It was more difficult for girls who knew no-one else and there were several who did not even know Norwich as they came from outlying parts of the county, travelling by train and bus, leaving home early in the mornings and arriving home about a couple of hours after the school day had ended.

We were very fortunate that our Form Mistress during our first year was Sister Theresa of the Holy Name. Young and bright with smiling brilliant blue eyes she welcomed us. We were allocated desks, smallest girls in the front rows, larger girls to the rear. Our desks soon filled with text-books and exercise books - the school providing sets for every pupil. When Margaret had started at the school the parents had had to provide all the books required. We were given our time-table. Lessons lasted 40 minutes each except when we had double periods for such subjects as needlework, art, and biology. Once settled in, the routine began.

One of our first lessons was French. A young, straight-from-university teacher bounced eagerly into the room. She wore a neat green costume under her University gown. Plump, with round rosy cheeks and a large smile, we liked her immediately.

'Bonjour, mes fillettes!' she started. 'Je m'appelle Ma'mselle Bangerter.' Then she proceeded to discover our names. Even when we found the subject difficult we enjoyed that year's French lessons. We longed for her to be our form mistress the following year but, much to our dismay, she had decided to become a nun and would be leaving us for another convent.

One of our early problems was being able to recognise the nuns from their back view. At first they all looked alike. One thing we did know was that having passed us they would not turn round. They must look straight ahead. Their habits consisted of long heavy black dresses, a head veil over a blinker-like headpiece with a white piece covering their foreheads and not a hair of their head could be seen. There was a large, very stiff white 'bib'. They wore thick black woollen stockings and flat black laced shoes. Their undergarments were enough to try the soul of a saint! Those of us from the prep. school described them to the others having sometimes seen the coarse dull blue bloomers drying on the convent linen line.

'Guessing the Nun' became quite a game during our early weeks.

There were only about half a dozen nuns actually teaching. We could soon recognise the slim tall back view of our own form-mistress by her sprightly step. The back view of 'Jimmy' was guessed from her small head and sloping shoulders. Sister Mary who taught needlework was also small but we soon realised that her head had a constant nodding movement. Sister Theresa of the Martyrs was tall but did not have the same happy spring in her step as our Sister Theresa had.There was another Sister Theresa, Sister Theresa Francis, whose rolling walk was unmistakeable and years before we entered the school had earned her the appropriate name of 'Ambulo', the Latin for 'I walk'. It became shortened to Amblo. Amblo taught Latin - and Classical Greek as an extra to keen pupils. She also took History and, of course, Religious Instruction. During my first year, there was also a nun in charge of the kitchen and I came to dread her more than the rest put together.

Which one is it?

School dinners were provided by the education authorities. The dining room was not large enough to hold all who wanted them and the first years had to use the cookery classroom. We sat on high stools by the cookery cupboards, sitting awkwardly sideways. Sister J. watched over us, giving orders when each group of four might join the queue and collect their dinners. Plates were provided but we had to take our own cutlery and white damask napkin and napkin ring, preferably silver, and kept polished! Girls whose mothers had given them bakelite or wooden ones felt definitely inferior - but, at least, they did not have to polish them!

One day during my first term I sat with three girls waiting for permission to go and collect our sweet course. We had finished the fish and potato pie. Whilst chatting to the others I had subconsciously seen a potato crumb on the table and idly flicked it with my fingers. To my horror and surprise it lifted off and hit Josephine sitting opposite right in the eye. She startled and jerked backwards. We laughed. I apologised. The episode could have finished there. It was an accident. But Sister J. thought otherwise.

'Stand up!' she ordered sharply. 'I saw you do that! Come here!'

I moved my stool and stood up facing the angry nun.

'What have you got to say for yourself?' she demanded.

'I am sorry, Sister.' I replied, standing contritely before her, eyes downcast.

'You are NOT!' she declared. 'You did it deliberately!'

'No Sister! I didn't, Sister. It was an accident. I am very sorry.'

'It was NOT an accident! You aimed it straight at Josephine's eye!'

Sister J's eyes were a hard, pale ice blue and her top lip sneered at me in my misery.

'Go and stand it that corner, facing the wall. You are not fit to eat with the others!' She indicated the corner where I was to stand. The rest of the children had gone silent whilst I received my telling off, but now began to speak in low whispers and soon conversation was back at its normal level. I felt sure everyone was looking at me but, no doubt, they soon had forgotten the hiatus and were busy eating their jam tart and custard. Whilst clearing the first course plates someone had dropped a plateful of potato on to the floor. The girl went to ask for a cloth, but Sister J. told her to leave it and summoned me from the corner to clear the sticky, slimy mess. Then it was back to face the wall again. The rest said grace and were dismissed. Sister J. ordered me to stand again before her. My knees were shaking but I was not going to let her see me cry. I fought back the tears.

'Fetch your second course.'

I collected a small piece of tart and sat down but had difficulty swallowing under her frosty stare. Eventually it was finished.

'Say your Grace!'

Struggling to remember the words of the 'Grace after meals' I started hesitantly, 'We give Thee thanks, Almighty God, for all Thy benefits ....,' and managed to stumble through to 'May the souls of the faithful departed, through the mercy of God, rest in peace. Amen.'

The cold eyes cut through me.

'I am very sorry, Sister,' I felt compelled to say, but Sister tightened her lips and refused to accept an apology.

'You will go and explain yourself to Sister St James on Monday. You may go now.'

Miserably I made my way to the playground. Playtime was nearly over. I felt sick throughout the afternoon and would not 'rest in peace' that night. In fact, so distressed was I by the whole incident that I became ill, had a fever and sore throat and a few days 'off sick'. Sister J. watched me closely when I returned and I had to work hard at doing nothing of which she might disapprove because she was ever ready to catch me again. She had made me very unhappy but, with hind-sight, I think she was a most unhappy person herself. She did not seem to get on with the other nuns and her stay at the convent was brief - thank goodness!

Not fit to eat with the others.

Cutting edges

Sister J. was not the only one with power to wither. The sewing mistress, was her equal any day.

After one of our first needlework lessons we were set homework 'to make a button-hole'. How she imagined we would know *how* to do it was a mystery, but, with Mother's guidance, I bound a hole with button-hole stitch. My friend had not managed to do more than cut a hole - she did not know where to start. She could have asked her grandmother, who was a tailoress, but she knew her grandmother would want to make a *perfect* button-hole and the teacher would know it was not her own effort. The mistress came round all the tables assessing our attempts. Her tongue could be as sharp as her dressmaker's scissors and, when she reached my friend and saw the hole in the material, unbound in any way, she nearly went hysterical.

'Look at this!' she shrieked. 'What do you call *this*?'

My friend stared at the ground wishing the floor would open.

'How many points do you expect for *that?*' she screamed. 'It's not worth *any* points! In fact I am giving you - *nought! Nought - minus!* '

Nought minus! We were too young and sensitive to see any funny side. Tears would be shed in private and the soreness of hurt feelings lasted for many years.

Our teacher certainly did not see anything funny about it.

Material was still difficult to obtain from the shops and clothing coupons were necessary, but our mothers had to find enough coupons and get material for us to turn into dresses. I went with Mother to several shops in the city to see what was available. We looked at the few bales of cottons in Bunting's and Garland's then climbed up Guildhall Hill to Chamberlin's, a somewhat superior store. All the assistants, wearing black dresses trimmed with white lace, stood silently by their counters. The shop-walker came towards us, asked our requirements, and detailed one of her underlings to attend to our needs - but that underling would not be allowed to actually take our money and coupons, only a *superior* could deal with that! Not having found anything suitable, we left the store, followed by the silent gaze of all the assistants. I was glad to escape from the most unnerving experience. Definitely not somewhere where one could browse round and see what was on offer, but very prestigious. We returned to Buntings and chose a material suitable for a first attempt, cotton, green with tiny red dots. The cutting-out took weeks of double periods, then I had not placed the pattern along a fold, so there was an extra seam centre front and back! Oh dear! There were only three sewing machines for the whole class. We could spend all of the double period queuing to show our work to the teacher and getting permission to proceed. If we carried on in the way *we* thought was correct the chances were it was not, and the next few lessons would be spent unpicking all we had done. Sewing progress was slow. So slow that, by the end of the year, my friend's dress was nowhere near completed. This time her grandmother, not wanting to see good material wasted and despite entreaties to leave it alone, insisted she would help and whisked the dress away and completed it. The perfect result did not please the infuriated teacher.

'And *who* did this?' she demanded, holding it aloft for all to see.

There were sighs of relief the following year when Sister Mary became our sewing mistress. She sat at a table in the centre of the room and one of us read aloud stories from Enid Blyton to keep us quiet whilst a queue formed to await instructions. Under Sister Mary's guidance we pieced together blouses and nightdresses, but in our fourth year needle-work was no longer included in our timetable.

'What do you call this?'

Scholarship

It must have been during my first term at the Notre Dame High School when I heard my parents talking about 'the scholarship'. Evidently my friend's father had made enquiries about new regulations concerning the 11+ examination. All children at State-run schools sat this examination to assess whether they would be suitable for Grammar School education. That one examination on that one fateful day in their lives decided their futures. Having been to a private first school, and having passed examinations to get in to the Notre Dame Preparatory School and another to get in to the Notre Dame High School, the thought that I might have to sit this examination never entered my head, but I was in for a shock.

'Well, what do you think?' Mother was asking as I entered the sitting-room.

'Yes.' Dad replied. 'I think Brennie might as well take it.' My father, sitting in his arm-chair by the fire, puffed at his pipe and looked up at me over the top of his glasses.

I looked from him to my mother and back to him again.

'What might I take?' I queried.

'The Scholarship.'

'What Scholarship?' I asked, but already my whole body was rushing with heat as I realised what they meant. Children who passed the Scholarship went to the Blyth School near Ebenezer House. It was a large school with a very strict headmistress. I did not like their uniform and blushed at thoughts of compulsory showers after games and physical education, in front of other girls and the gym mistresses. They played hockey, too. I did *not* want to go there.

'What is the matter?' Dad asked, seeing my miserable expression.

'But I don't want to take the scholarship. I don't want to go to the Blyth School!' I declared.

'Your Mother was talking to Mr H. this morning. It seems you would not have to go to the Blyth School. You could still remain at the Notre Dame. There are Scholarship girls in your class aren't there?'

'Yes,' I answered. 'But I don't see why I should take the exam. Margaret didn't!'

'It is different now,' Dad explained. 'The Government have brought in new laws.'

Bother the Government! I did NOT, repeat NOT want to sit the 11+. I was just beginning to feel settled in at school. Bother Mr H.! Bother the City Hall!

I went outside and sat on my swing. Higher and higher I made it go. Then I thought about my friend. What would she think? Would she feel as angry as I did? What difference would it make, anyway? I did not enjoy that weekend. On the Monday we discussed our problem. It seemed we could take the examination and benefit from free schooling - provided, of course, that we passed. If we did not pass we stayed as we were and our parents would continue to pay. What if we tried to fail?

Friday 6th February 1948 was the dreaded day.

Margaret left for school as usual. Dad left for the shop.

'I hope you get on all right.' They had both said before leaving.

I began to have butterflies in my tummy. Mother was busy getting ready to bath my baby sister. I watched.

'Do you think I should go now?' I asked more than once.

'You don't want to get there too soon. Wait a bit longer.'

I wandered about the house. Eventually Mother said, 'I should think you might as well put your coat on now.'

At last I had something positive to do. My raincoat on and school hat in place, I went into the kitchen, pulling on my brown kid gloves.

'Which school have I got to go to?' I asked, suddenly realising I did not know and both local schools were within walking distance.

'Oh dear!' Mother stopped what she was doing and looked at me in horror. 'I don't know. I don't think your Father said.'

I felt sick. It had not been mentioned. Mother could see I was near tears. She thought for a few moments then came to the conclusion that it was at the Secondary Modern School at Recreation Ground Road. Children who did not pass the scholarship went there.

'There's no need to run. You have got just nice time. Mind how you cross Wroxham Road.' She gave an encouraging smile. 'Good Luck! Do your best!'

'Bye!' I called as I closed the front door and set off down Blackwell Avenue and along Fairstead Road. At the main Wroxham Road I stopped. The early morning rush of bicycles and cars was over and there was nothing in sight except for two red double-decker buses following each other. The number 9 going from Wroxham to Norwich 'Bus Station and the 91 from

Sprowston Blue Boar to Tombland and on to Norwich Thorpe Railway Station passed me. I wished I could be on one of them instead of crossing the road towards the school.

I was not sure which entrance to go through, not being familiar with the building. One of the doors was open and led into a long corridor where brick 'blast walls' built during the war were still jutting across the passageway. Everywhere was extremely quiet. Perhaps the exam had started. I caught sight of someone pushing a large broom. It was the caretaker, Mr. Elphinstone. I knew him. He had made our birthday cakes for years. He looked puzzled to see me.

'Hello!' he said, 'What are you doing here?'

'I've come to take the scholarship.'

'Oh dear!' he took off his hat and scratched his head. 'It's not here you ought to be. They are all down at the other school.'

He took a watch from his pocket and shook his head.

'They'll be startin' any minute now. Make you haste, Missy, you've got no time to lose!' For a moment I stared at him in disbelief and he stared back, then he said urgently,

'Hurry you along, Missy. If you are quick you may just be in time.'

'Make you haste, Missy.'

How my legs carried me along Wroxham Road and into School Lane I shall never know. They were shaking like jelly. I felt sick and my chest hurt when I ran and my legs ached when I walked. At last the school was in sight. A lady was coming out of the gates on her bicycle. I knew her son, Norman, as we had been at Miss Bidewell's together.

'Where have you been?' she demanded. 'They have been looking for you. Hurry up.'

There was no time to answer. I stumbled through the door.

'Elsie Sayle?' someone asked. It sounded strange to be called by my first name.

I nodded in reply, unable to speak. The lady called through to someone else in the examination room,

'She's here!' And, turning to me, she snapped,

'You have kept everyone waiting. Hang your coat and hat on that hook. Now, come and sit down - there.'

All the other children turned to look at me. I felt terrible. Coming in late made me conspicuous enough but I soon realised I was the only one wearing a school uniform. I felt dreadfully self-conscious. But there wasn't time to take breath before books of questions were placed before us. My mouth was dry, my eyes were watering. I would have loved a drink of water. It was several seconds before my eyes would focus on the printed page and I started answering questions. Some of the arithmetical problems were like a foreign language; I had heard of bushels and pecks, quarts and gallons, feet and yards, rods, poles or perches but - whatever were quires and reams?

At last, it was all over. The person in charge was still complaining about me being late.

'Whatever happened to you?' Norman's mother asked when she came to collect him. Several of the mothers were looking at me.

'Oh dear! Fancy going to the wrong school! She had to run all that way!' she passed my explanation on to the women.

'Poor little thing!' said one of them.

It seemed a long walk up Mousehold Lane, but at last I turned in to Blackwell Avenue.

'How did you get on?' Mother asked as soon as I walked indoors.

'It was at the other school!'

'What?' she gasped.

'It was at School Lane School,' I told her.

'Oh no!' she exclaimed. 'Oh no! It was my fault for not checking with your father. I ought to have asked him before he left for work. Oh poor Brennie!'

At that moment Dad's car came in to the drive. Before he could ask about my morning Mother said,

'You never told me which school. She went to the wrong one!'

'What do you mean? Hasn't she done the exam.?'

'Yes. But she went to the wrong school and only got there just in time. Poor little thing, she's all in.'

They spent much of the mealtime discussing (they never really argued) how there had been a misunderstanding.

'Never mind, Brennie!' Dad said. 'It's over now. You can forget about it.'

It does not surprise me that the entry in Mother's diary for the following day records that I was unwell.

It was not until the 14th June that Mother's diary entry reads: 'Heard B. has passed scholarship, 1st part.' There was a *second* part!

The second part was an interview with an educational official. Dad took me in the car to Stracey Road, Thorpe. After waiting for a short time I was called in to a big room where two men sat behind a dark, heavy desk. They presented me with a type-written piece of prose from, presumably, Seaman Yeo's tales - at least, that is what was written at the top. I read through this and answered questions. They were quite kindly but I was glad to escape.

Two weeks later confirmation came that I had passed and been granted a scholarship for . . the Blyth School! I could *not* have a free place at Notre Dame as I had not attended a state school for at least two years. The same applied to my friend. Our parents had been wrongly advised. Letters went to the Education Authorities and even to the Minister for Education all to no avail. We definitely could *not* have a free place at Notre Dame and the fees at that time were nine guineas a term. The Blyth School was an equally good school, but we were glad our parents decided we could stay where we were already settled.

All that stressful effort for nothing!

Second Year

The 'jolly' French teacher having left obviously she could not be our form mistress for the second year. We were to have Miss H. who taught mathematics throughout the upper school. In our first year we had been taught mathematics by a nun who either did not understand the subject herself or was simply unable to convey the facts to us. We learned nothing in that first year and finished thoroughly confused as to the different meanings of, for example, $2x$ and x^2. As we progressed up the school we were frequently reminded that the year below us was further through the syllabus than we were. They just cannot have had such a disastrous start.

Miss H. was tall and thin with grey wavy hair held neatly back in a bun. Smartly dressed and upright, she walked briskly into the classroom on her size nine laced-up leather shoes (size nine for *ladies* shoes was almost unheard of at that time) and at the heels of those shoes came her little dog, Ricky, a black and white terrier. Of course, Ricky was a great distraction, especially when he decided he wanted to sit on a particular girl's chair. How could a twelve year old concentrate on angles and Pythagoras with a dog fidgeting behind her? Ricky was very partial to rubbers, too, and as these were not easily obtainable, girls tried to keep them hidden from view, but, naturally, he could sniff them out and many disappeared down his throat.

New subjects entered our time-table. We started to learn Latin and, like many previous generations, chanted 'amo, amas, amat' and 'hic, haec, hoc' et cetera. Transference of knowledge depends so much on teacher/pupil relationship and my rapport with this one left a lot to be desired. It was not long before I had to join the sad little line of sinners waiting to be admonished by Jimmy for getting three detentions for poor work. Not all the 'sinners' were there for bad work, in fact, it was usually for unacceptable behaviour; *dreadful* sins such as having been seen talking to a *boy* - even if that particular boy was the girl's own brother! Perhaps the girl had been seen *eating a sweet* on the 'bus, or *talking* along the corridor, or *not* wearing indoor shoes when indoors or *not* wearing a hat or gloves when in the street. So deeply planted in our consciences were these rules that when one of my friends, years later, married and pushing her baby along the pavement in a pram, happened to see the senior mistress coming towards her, she

Sad little line of sinners

experienced real panic because *she was not wearing gloves*! So trivial were some of our 'crimes' that we sometimes felt justified in fabricating a white lie - it saved so much hassle. Occasionally it was possible to walk along the corridors during playtime when everyone *ought* to be outside and, by assuming a legitimately purposeful air, not be challenged. Another friend recalls how, whilst walking along a corridor, she met a nun coming in the opposite direction. There was no opportunity to escape so, head held high, she continued walking, fully expecting to be quizzed on her reasons for being indoors, instead, she was astounded to hear the nun praise her for walking in single file, 'That's right,' said the nun, 'keep to single file.' My friend looked all around her to see the rest of the file, but, as she thought, there was none - she was all alone!

One lunch hour, for some reason now forgotten, I was 'in' when I ought to have been 'out' and was just creeping down the stairs when a nun emerged from the Headmistress's corridor. I froze.

'Well, Madam,' she said, licking her lips and looking down at me, 'what are you doing here? Why are you not in the play-ground?' She sniffed.

Self-preservation rushed to my aid. This particular nun was in charge of the 'Holy Shop' and *we were standing right beside it*. I had a few spare pennies in my strap-purse so I smiled up at the nun and asked politely,

'Please, Sister, can you tell me when the Holy Shop will be open?'

The tall nun's expression changed, she drew a large, blue check duster-

'Well Madam, what are you doing here?'

like handkerchief from her pocket, wiped her nose then licked her lips before replying,

'Well, Madam,' (she always addressed us as Madam) 'is there something you particularly want?' She smiled encouragingly.

I looked through the glass doors at the rosaries, the crucifixes, missals, statuettes and holy pictures. Having only a few coppers I selected a small card bearing a religious text to do with forgiveness of sin, paid for it and, thankfully, escaped to the playground trusting that *my* latest sin would be forgiven.

This year, instead of biology we had general science, and one lesson, at least, could have had serious consequences as the jam-jar containing magnesium *exploded* during a demonstration to show what happens when a match is applied to magnesium. We saw only too clearly what happens! An unforgettable lesson.

Then there was theory of music and appreciation of music which most of us did not appreciate. How many eleven to twelve year-olds could understand Thomas Tallis or Purcell? How we longed for the bell to ring at the end of lessons especially on dark winter afternoons.

In the gymnasium we did country dancing, usually 'I lost my stocking in the brook', or we played volley ball or worked on the apparatus. I was never much good at games and volley ball required a certain amount of aggressiveness and height, although in the second year, but *only* in the second year, I actually *enjoyed* the sessions spent with the wall bars, the window-frame, the vaulting horse, the beam and the ropes and was one of the few to climb to the top. Perhaps that helped my position in class because, from being 'somewhere in the middle' I rose to fifth place. It felt good when time came for 'semi-circles'.

'Semi-circles' took place at the end of every term in the main Assembly Hall. It was a dreadful ordeal, especially for anyone who did not achieve good results. Each form was called forth in turn and in front of other classes their results were read out. Those gaining distinction (over 70%) went to the front. Behind them those gaining credit (over 50%) formed a semi-circle round them. Then those with passes (over 40%) formed another semi-circle and those with failures stood forlornly at the back. Some gained medals or badges for particular subjects and ascended the stairs to the stage to receive them from the head mistress. Comments were addressed to the form by the headmistress and the girls were allowed back to their normal place in the Hall. Then the next form and the next and so on. Until we went into the Hall we did not know our class place. It was a dreadful feeling to be left at the back until very few of one's class remained, as I experienced one term in my fourth year, having been absent for all the examinations, and our placing was an average of the marks for both term work and examinations. Consequently I was 33rd out of 34 with an average mark of 40%. The headmistress turned to our form mistress and asked,

'And what is Brenda doing there? Why is her position so low?'

I felt utterly disgraced - but I had not *asked* to be ill.

The same thing happened another year. I had not sought out German measles, in fact they took me completely by surprise. Looking in a mirror to make sure my school hat was on straight one morning I realised my face was covered with a rash. Mother took one look,

'You cannot go to school like that. You had better call in at the doctor's and see what he says.'

I got off the 'bus at the doctor's surgery and squeezed my way inside. It was a tiny waiting-room with a wooden bench around the walls and, as usual in the early days of the National Health Service, every inch was occupied. It was necessary to notice who was there when one went in because woe betide anyone who tried to see the doctor out of turn! I sat there wearing my school uniform and clutching my case of homework books. Eventually my turn came.

'Good morning, Doctor,' I said in answer to his cheery greeting. The doctor was always full of bounce and so quick that his stethoscope had listened in to a chest almost before the patient could remove the necessary clothes and people felt sure he had written out their prescription before they had even entered the room. 'I have got a rash,' I continued hesitantly, 'and wonder if it is anything infectious?'

He put his hands around my neck to feel the glands, peered at me through his spectacles, twitched his moustache and declared,

'I should say it is! A fortnight at home for you. You have got rubella - German measles.'

I left his surgery feeling like an untouchable and walked home, keeping my distance from all people along the route.

Family doctors were not the only doctors we saw. Annual visits were paid to the school by the school doctor. All pupils, subject to parent's or guardian's consent, could have a free medical examination. Thoroughly checked over, our age, weight and height noted, our sight was tested and advice was given.One year the school doctor decided I had flat feet and I joined the 'flat-footed Fanny parade' doing exercises under the supervision of our gym mistress. My grandfather's flat feet had excluded him from being accepted for the army in the 1914-18 war but, although the authorities thought he would not able to march, there was a time when he walked seven miles to work, was on his feet all day, then walked seven miles home at night without any problems.

We received our reports on the last day of each term. They were in a hard-backed book bearing the school crest and had to be signed by our parents, who undoubtedly would comment upon our results and the teachers remarks, especially the 'could do better' ones. The books were re-turned to the school at the start of the next term.

The last day of each term was memorable for something other than academic results - it was the day when desks were cleaned and polished. Armed with cloths and polishing rags, a small bottle of vinegar, Brasso and our mothers' best furniture polish we prepared for action, rubbing away the ink-spots with the vinegar and polishing until we had exhausted our supply of elbow-grease. Surely the smell of polish and vinegar must evoke in every ex-pupil from those days the bustle and hubbub of the last day of term.

During term time, but extra to the syllabus, we were able to take elocution lessons or violin lessons. I had elocution once or twice a week during the lunch time. Sister Theresa of the Holy Name was very good and enthusiastic. Happily we chorused 'How now brown cow' and 'Two new blue balloons', but were less happy when the time came to enter the oral examinations. Set pieces had to be memorised and recited to the examiner's satisfaction and there was sight-reading to cope with, too. My favourite exam piece was 'The Duck and the Kangaroo' which gained me a distinction for Grade One. Edward Lear's poetry was often used. Besides individual elocution lessons the school was very keen to enter whole classes for Choral Speaking at the Norfolk County Music Festival. T. S. Eliot's 'Jellicle Cats' was the chosen poem one year. Evidently our mothers, in the audience, had difficulty controlling their laughter at our expressive red faces as we rattled away - and earned first place. The school was proud of its record at the Festival.

The school was also justly proud of the netball team which held the County Shield for many years. Games, netball and tennis, accounted for many hours of extra-curricular activity and competition between local schools was fierce. The main problems came from lack of equipment, not because the school would not provide it, but because, even post-war, there were shortages nationwide. In our first year, tennis racquets had been ordered for us (and paid for by our parents), but they did not arrive at the school until the *last week* of the summer term. In the meantime we had had many lessons learning to 'shake hands with our rackets' and had been shown various strokes. It was quite an experience to 'shake hands' with the actual tool at last but, even though we were late getting the equipment to use at school, many happy hours would be spent with our friends on the courts of local parks during the long summer holiday. Often we went by 'bus to Eaton Park at the other side of Norwich where there were dozens of courts, grass and hard, but sometimes the demand for them was so great we had to wait hours before we could get a game. Every year we tried to get to Eaton Park, not to play, but to watch the progress of players through the Parks Tennis Tournaments and stayed as long as possible watching them battle it out in the fading light. It might not be Wimbledon, but we had never been *there* and, before the arrival of television, we had no means of comparison. Anyhow, it was excellent entertainment.

Growing up

Mother's diary records on 2nd September 1949 that 'Brenda goes into long stockings for school', a landmark worthy of note and almost as momentous for girls as the transition from short to long trousers must have been for boys. Until then it had been brown knee-socks and elastic garters. Mothers were always knitting socks or mending them. Outgrown woollies were pulled out, the wool re-wound and re-used time and again in order to save precious clothing coupons. Even socks needed coupons from the allowance of only sixty-six coupons for a whole year, and clothing coupons were issued until 1949. But from now on it was to be stockings and suspender belts. Not *nylon* stockings because they were only just coming on to the market - and occasionally could be found at the back of Norwich Market where a couple of 'spivs', Mike and Bernie Winters, came from London with supplies and entertained the crowd. In the shops a supply of nylons resulted in long queues and was soon gone. Behind the big windows of dry-cleaners young women sat ruining their eyesight as they worked small machines and repaired ladders in nylons at a shilling or so per inch and there were queues waiting to collect the repairs. People took great care of their nylons. We had to take equal care of our 'bullet-proofs' our lisle stockings, or, maybe, we had rayon stockings. We were unlikely to have silk ones for school. Whatever they were made of they all had *seams* and the seams *must be straight!* It was incredible that those seams, straight when we set off for school, could so quickly twist themselves around the leg almost to the front. We wanted to feel grown up, but often longed for the less troublesome knee socks, though, even with them, there had been useless garters or missing garters and no elastic to make any more. Stockings were *not* easy! During the war they had been impossible to get, and women had resorted to covering their legs with a brown liquid make-up which looked terrible when it rained.

Our English mistress mentioned *her* stockings one day which took us by surprise because, until then, we had not really thought of her having *legs*! It came about as a result of our first exercise in lovely new exercise books. Someone had written an essay and had failed to use any full stops. The mistress explained that it was a good idea to stop sometimes and do something else, for instance, she might stop correcting essays and wash some stockings! Well! Well! She *was* human after all! Human but *very* superior! She evidently had not enjoyed marking the work of one of the other forms. Their marked exercise books had preceded her one day, some small girl, endeavouring to gain a point for her house, having staggered in under the weight of them. She had followed, swooping in to their classroom, academic gown slightly off one shoulder as was her wont, seated herself at the teacher's desk, removed the elastic band from her pencil case of well-sharpened pencils, dabbed at her nose with her handkerchief and described how she coped when marking their work.

'When I am marking your essays,' she told them, 'I keep some chocolates by me so I may eat one to take away the nasty taste.'

She was very good at the 'put down'. Often, when a pupil attempted to answer a question, she would say,

'Well of course, my dear, you are entitled to your own opinion but *I* think. . .' and we knew who had the better opinion, *didn't we*?

Some small girl having staggered under the weight of them

Our form-mistress at this time was none other than Amblo, and, in a way, we grew rather fond of her.

Our cloakrooms were 'wire cages' and always left open, but only very rarely was anything stolen from there. Our satchels or cases, our coats, hats, gloves, shoes, gym wear, tennis rackets, violins had to be left there until needed. We each had a shoe bag which *must* be taken home with us on Fridays, the intention being that we should clean our indoor shoes and gym shoes as well as our outdoor ones, of course. There was no chance not to take them when Amblo stood and reminded each one of us as we said 'Good night, Sister'.

'Good night. Have you got your shoe bag?'

'Good night. Don't forget your shoe bag!'

'Have you got your shoe bag?

Muffled up and laden down with homework, perhaps a violin or tennis racquet too, we bowed as we passed her and left the cloakrooms. Her voice could still be heard, gradually growing fainter as we made our way to the school gate.

'Have you got your shoe bag? Don't forget your shoe bag.'

Those shoe bags - they haunted us!

Never one to linger longer than necessary at school I hurried down Surrey Street, past the bombed remains of the ancient Boar's Head and across the narrow St Stephen's Street, where a policeman was usually on point duty, then ran over the Woolworth's bombed site, crossed Rampant Horse Street to Brigg Street to await the 'bus. Why had I hurried? Often for no good reason because there could be a long wait. Sometimes huge queues formed and a great cheer would go up as the 'bus appeared edging its way along the narrow street between the tall dark-red brick buildings further up the hill. Some of the 'buses had seen better days and, once, after a dreadfully long wait the men in the queue could not believe their eyes,

'Cor! Wherever have they found *that*?" they chortled, 'It's an old 'Tiger'!' and the antiquated single-deck vehicle rattled to a stop. Everyone pressed inside like sardines in a tin and we chugged home.

'Buses had drivers and conductors (or conductresses during the war), the conductors pushing their way past the packed passengers to collect fares. After a long period when my fare had been threepence it was increased by a penny and I well remember blushing scarlet the first time I asked for a 'fourpenny one'!

'I'll give you a fourpenny one!' teased the conductor, much to everyone's amusement except mine.

But my embarrassment was nothing compared to that of a girl from another school. This girl had sat on one of the seats which faced each other just inside the 'bus and, evidently, she used a season ticket. No sooner had she settled on her seat than the young male conductor swung down the stairs and asked to see her ticket. She started to blush and no wonder because she kept it in her knicker pocket! What a job she had trying to lift her skirt, undo the pocket button and produce the required ticket under the attentive gaze of the conductor. By the time he had been satisfied her face was as red as the 'bus itself.

Sometimes after school I did not wait at Brigg Street for a 'bus but hurried through Brigg Street between bombed out shops on one side and the huge water tank which filled the bomb site of Curls, one of the largest stores of Norwich. Now that the war was over, the tank was to be drained and there was much speculation about what would be found in there and whether there were any fish or eels. Definitely there were eels in a fresh water tank under the fish slabs of the Mac Fisheries shop on The Walk and I always took a quick sympathetic look at them as I passed.

Then my steps took me past Green's the Outfitters, where we went to be measured for our school uniforms. Past J. F. Collin the Chemist, where my parents had met in the 1920s. Past the entrance to The Royal Arcade, past jewellers and the bank and further on to Hope Bros. on the corner of London Street, its windows displaying high quality goods. Across London Street on the opposite corner was Jarrolds, or what was usable of it at that time. Once I hurried there just to get a pencil *with paint on it.* Someone at school had bought one and, after the plain utility War Drawing pencils, this was worth going out of one's way for and I was lucky! Quite often it was necessary to go to Jarrolds to get a new nib for a fountain pen - or, even to have the nib uncrossed. And, when in the shop, I always looked at the tiny corner where a few books were on the shelves. During the war, books were very scarce indeed and of very poor quality paper, but gradually books were appearing and I was thrilled when I saw a few Observers' Books on the shelf behind the assistant. My first purchase was *The Observers' Book of Wild Flowers* which, I believe, cost three shillings and sixpence. I spent hours studying it, trying to memorise the names of flowers so that I might recognise them. Some were already familiar to me as Dad was knowledgeable about botany and had taught me quite a lot. Other Observers' Books were bought as they were available and as pocket money would permit. Pocket money was, possibly, a shilling a week at that time and there were other things to buy - especially when Diane was recovering from pneumonia. She had been very ill, and antibiotics were not then in use although sulphonamides were. However, she was getting better and, by then, the Woolworth's store had been rebuilt on the bomb site so, instead of scrambling over the rubble, I walked through the smart, new shop and sought out brightly-coloured jigsaw puzzles featuring Snow White scenes from the Walt Disney film. Of course we did them time and again, but I got much pleasure from doing them with her, especially as, until then, we had only had jigsaws surviving from pre-war days. My own memories of Snow White had been of nightmares following an outing to the Haymarket in August 1944, where we saw the film and heard the blood-curdling scream of the old witch as she fell over the cliff!

Occasionally I went in another direction by the Cattle Market and made my way down to Wick's Pet Shop to get food for my four goldfish. Climbing the steep steps and going into that shop was an education! Loud macaws greeted the customers and there were cages full of rabbits, mice, kittens, tortoises; everything imaginable was crammed in there! The overwhelming smell of meal and animals brimmed over down the steep steps on to the pavement. Behind the counter, a lady, red-faced as her parrots, dispensed advice on animal care as she weighed up the orders and gave details of the origin of the horse-meat she was cutting up.

'Comes from Argentina, my dear,' she announced for all to hear. 'Wild horses. Nothing but the best.'

Goldfish did not need horse-meat, thank goodness. Poor wild horses!

Once out of the shop, I walked quickly past The Buff Coat Public House and down to Norwich Thorpe Railway Station Yard where all the 'buses terminated.

The 'bus route home went through the narrow Magdalen Street and, although there was not a great amount of traffic, apart from bicycles, the 'bus was brought to a halt on occasion by bullocks or sheep being driven from the Cattle Market out to the country.

Many years later, in 1991, I sat at the front of the top deck of a 'bus leaving Norwich via Magdalen Street. Beside me a young boy was enthusiastically doing his history homework. He had been to see the new building developments taking place on the old Cattle Market which, since 1961 had been nothing more than a car-park. He told me there used to be a Cattle Market there.

'Yes,' I replied, 'I can remember that.' Then I thought I would tell him about the hold-ups of traffic in Magdalen Street in those days.

'When I used to come home from school on a 'bus like this, sometimes the 'bus had to stop because the road was blocked. Can you think why it was blocked?'

He shook his head.

'Because a flock of sheep or some bullocks or cows were being driven along by farmers taking them to the country.'

He looked at me with wide eyes.

'How old are you?' I asked.

'Nine,' came the reply.

'Well, I was about nine then and I am fifty-five now, so that's how long ago it was. It does not seem long ago to me but nobody would try to drive sheep along here now, would they?'

His eyes grew very big and I supposed he was imagining the sheep and cows but he smiled thoughtfully as he stared hard at me and asked incredulously,

'Aren't you *too old* to be travelling on a 'bus?'

So innocently he put me in my historic place!

Television

Unlike Margaret, who often stayed for after-school activities, I always hurried home from school, especially in the winter months when it was dark and cold. Indoors I knew Mother would be waiting with Diane, who, from the age of three and a half went to St Christopher's School at Old Catton in the mornings. When Diane was five she started at the Notre Dame Preparatory School, and then I could not possibly be late, for often I brought her home with me.

Sometimes there might be a slight draw-back to being home so punctually as, after trailing up Mousehold Lane, relieved to open the door and see Mother sitting by the fire, possibly knitting or mending, she would greet me with,

'You're just the girl I need. Before you take your coat off, just fill the coal scuttle. It will save your poor old Dad when he gets home. There's an Izry on the hall stand.'

'You're just the girl I need.'

Giving a little groan, (but only a little one!) I put down my case full of homework books and picked up the torch. We always called torches 'Izries' and it was years before I discovered why - it was short for 'Israelite', but our torch with tired battery was anything but the 'light of the world'. Dimly it flickered in the coal shed and we had to guess where the coals were and try to forget the large spiders lurking there!

No homework was done by me on Friday nights because I had joined the St John Ambulance Brigade and the meetings were on Fridays in Sprowston Church Hall. Margaret was in the Guides but, because I had always wanted to become a nurse, it was decided to encourage me towards first aid and nursing. At that time Sprowston was *the* best detachment in the area. With the enthusiastic Diana Grenville in charge we won many competitions. We drilled smartly in our uniforms and took a variety of examinations; First Aid, Home Nursing, Child Welfare, Hygiene, etc. We paraded at Church Parades and, one year, were reviewed by H.R.H. Princess Margaret at Sennowe Park. How blue her eyes! How hot the sun - so hot one of our group fainted as soon as the Princess passed. It was through St John that I got some first-hand experience of nursing by working for my 200 hour hospital badge at the local children's hospital on Sunday afternoons. School homework had to be squeezed into Saturday. The amount of homework increased as we progressed up the school. In the first year it was about one hour and I can remember the struggle to learn the Catechism and the parables in order to be able to write them out, word perfect, the following day. Without central heating, but with fuel shortages and cold weather the whole family would spend the evening in the one warm room, so concentration was difficult. But in order to allow us to concentrate as much as possible Mother and Dad would not even listen to the wireless until our work was done.

Before long, however, there would be an even more intrusive medium than wireless, as we were to discover during our Easter holidays in 1950 when we went to visit Grandfather at Huntingdon. We travelled by way of Downham Market to visit other relations en route. In places as we went through Fenland we could see the full rivers lapping the tops of the banks which were high above the road. It was rather frightening to think what might happen if those banks gave way as they had in 1947. It was the first time I had actually seen the *black fens*. Learning about places and peoples and the conditions in which they live from a book, as we did in geography lessons, was not nearly as good as seeing for ourselves. Until I went to the Lake District in 1954 I had no idea how *wet* mountains could be. But, that Easter we saw something for the first time which was to alter everyone's knowledge of the world, *Television!*

Grandfather Sayle was one of the first people in Huntingdon to have a set. That fact that he lived in the High Street, which was part of the old Ermine Street, the A1 Road, where traffic, without suppressors, was increasing rapidly, did not really help our initial impressions. The small nine-inch screen flickered a snowstorm most of the time and whenever a vehicle went past, a solid bar of light rolled up the screen accompanied by an ear-splitting buzz. Occasionally glimpses of the young Petula Clark or Muffin the Mule could be deciphered provided the curtains were closed to keep out the light. Mother's reaction, voiced on the car journey home was,

'That dreadful television! Switched on for hours, warming up before the programmes start, and with the curtains drawn! All those war years we had to have black-out - why shut out the sunshine now?'

Fascinating as it was, it had spoiled our holiday.

'I expect it will improve,' Dad replied, but he had been irritated by it too.

'I hope so!' retorted Mother. 'Because if it doesn't I do not want it! There was no chance for conversation or anything - not even a game of cards!'

A game of cards was traditional at Grandfather's and Mother looked forward to playing Solo Whist. Sometimes, in winter evenings, they played at home with the neighbours and, occasionally, when they noticed boredom creeping over us, would suggest we got out the pack of cards. Usually we played Sevens or Newmarket (using cob nuts rather than money to back our 'horses') but, as we grew older we were taught how to play whist.

Unfortunately that was to cause me a great embarrassment when I was about fourteen. My older sister and I were staying with our relations at Downham Market when they asked if we could play whist. Imagining they wanted a quiet game that evening we replied, 'Yes.'

'That is good!' said our aunt enthusiastically, 'there is a Conservative Whist Drive at the Major's tomorrow evening. We can all go.'

Our hearts sank. We knew we were not up to that standard but our protests fell on deaf ears and the following evening we were taken to the Major's. Perhaps two dozen people had already arrived and were settling

NOTRE DAME HIGH SCHOOL

(Photographs by courtesy of A.E.Coe & Sons Ltd.)

The School exterior

The Assembly Hall

A Classroom

NOTRE DAME HIGH SCHOOL

(Photographs by courtesy of A.E.Coe & Sons Ltd.)

The Laboratory.

The Gymnasium.

The Domestic Science Classroom.

County Champions! The Netball Team 1952.

N.D.H.S. Dramatic Society in 'She Stoops to Conquer'.

'Breaking-up Day' July 1952. Form V with Miss Francis.

'Leaving Day' July 1953. Form V with Sister Theresa Francis.

themselves at card tables. Some of them, no doubt, lived and breathed whist and bridge, their eyes did not miss a single spot and, when I played a wrong card during the first game, those eyes burned through me.

'She's revoked!' they cried in horror, and the whole assembly turned to see who could have done such a thing. If only this could be just a nightmare but it was all too painfully real as I had to progress around the room and could feel the dismay emanating from the other players as I moved on to their table. Never again would I go to a whist drive! Certainly I would never again be invited to one run by that particular Conservative Association.

Glimpses of Muffin the Mule

195a Sprowston Road

Spring school holidays often coincided with 'spring-cleaning' which included having the chimneys swept after the winter fires. For years we had the same sweep, a quiet man with an unfortunate stutter. Curtains taken down, mats lifted, all furniture covered by newspapers and newspapers spread all over the floors we waited for him to arrive on his bicycle; rods and brushes strapped on his carrier. As sweeps went he was a 'clean' sweep, but somehow the soot got everywhere. When small we were sent outside to watch for the brush to come out of the chimney-pot, accompanied by a shower of soot making us shout excitedly. The brush gave a little shake, disappeared inside the chimney-pot, popped out again, gave another little shake and was gone. When more than one chimney was being swept we had a repetition of the excitement. Usually the sweep left a bucketful of soot 'for the garden' which was to keep slugs from the lettuces. After he had gone, and the soot-dust settled, there was a lot of hard work cleaning up. The smell of soot lingered for some time but, at least, the smell was preferable to that which pervaded the air when cesspools were being emptied. Before mains drainage was installed cesspools had to be emptied quite often. A tanker-lorry came to empty them (in some villages the outdoor privy buckets were still being emptied by men and the 'night soil' cart, certainly until the late 1960s, possibly in to the 1970's). The smell was dreadful. Some of the houses in Mousehold Lane needed their communal cesspool emptied every few weeks and, when this was in progress, we covered our noses with handkerchiefs and rushed up the lane as fast as we could. Mains drainage was a real boon.

The brush gave a little shake..

Another of the council's services was, of course, refuse collection. Men emptied dustbins into open, oval zinc baths which they hoisted on to their shoulders, resting them on leather reinforcements on their jackets, then hurrying along garden paths to the waiting lorry. They always worked as fast as they could, making plenty of noise in the process and, on windy days, left a trail of paper and used 'bus-tickets strewn along the gutters and caught up in the hedges, but much of a dustbin's content in those days was ash and cinders from open fires, not much paper and scarcely any packaging or tins. Anything salvageable was salvaged in war-time.

In our eight-week-long summer holidays we spent much time in the garden practising tennis strokes on a "Kum-Bak" (where a tennis ball was fastened to strong elastic suspended between two wooden poles held upright by guy-ropes); we had many happy hours just reading to, or playing with, our little sister as we rocked in a Ministry of Defence surplus naval hammock slung beneath two apple trees in the orchard and, of course, we helped Mother preparing food, shopping and cleaning. When old enough, we helped Dad in the shop, too. At first it was somewhat nerve-racking standing behind the counter facing customers. Knowing where everything was kept could only come with experience and by being observant when doing the daily dusting. Many items were kept in glass-fronted show-cases. There were numerous cough remedies such as Glycerine, Lemon and Honey for dry coughs; Lemon, Honey and *Borax* for productive coughs, many proprietary brands and, my favourite, Sayle's Bronchial Mixture for Children. It was many years before some of the ingredients, for example Borax, were declared unsafe. Shelves were stacked with baby-foods, Trufood, Ostermilk, Cow & Gate and gradually the little tins of prepared baby meals, and there was Woodward's Gripe Water. Baby scales were in frequent use as mothers regularly checked the weight of their babies where they themselves may have been weighed by their own mothers. Beside perfumes and lipsticks stood talcum powders and soaps and drawers full of packets of powdered shampoos, Stablonde, Brunitex, Icilma, Amami and many more before the influx of liquid shampoos. Later shelf-room had to be found to display the home-perms such as Pin-up, Toni or Richard Hudnut, as that craze swept through. I became quite good at doing them myself and was in demand by family and friends.

The early days of the National Health Service meant an enormous increase in dispensing as everybody rushed to obtain free medicines. The doctor's waiting room was overflowing and the patients left happily clutching their 'susscription' and piled into the chemists' shops where they waited, often impatiently, as most of the medicines were dispensed as required. Ointments could take quite a time to make up and patients were often asked to collect those later. Some frequently prescribed mixtures could be made up and kept in large Winchester quart bottles. Several of these stood on shelves behind the dispensing counter bearing their labels such as, Mist. Mag. Trisil., Mist Ammon. Chlor., and, of course, Sayle's Bronchial Mixture for Children amongst the rest. Mist Ammon. Chlor. was *ghastly* and, over the years, we must have swallowed pints of the 'black stuff' to cure coughs. Gradually more medicines were obtainable ready prepared and there was a huge increase in the number of sedatives prescribed. Special cupboards were made to house all the barbiturates and even more cupboards when antibiotics appeared on the scene.

Not all medicines were available only on prescription but some were best supervised by a pharmacist. I remember one elderly lady, who lived just around the corner from the shop, shuffling in wearing her slippers and, almost every day, asking for tubes of a proprietary sleeping tablet. A tactful word with her doctor was called for. The poor old lady was perpetually half asleep trying to blot out her problems.

Then there were those who came in for 'a penn'orth' (a penny-worth) of Beecham's pills or a twist of Bile Beans, two tiny pills in a twist of paper. There were cascara pills and liver pills and all sorts of torments for bowels, and glycerine suppositories in sizes suitable for infants, children and adults. People were obsessed with such things. One local trader came in last thing at the end of the week, every week, for 'a draught' to keep him 'reg'lar'. Standing beside the dispensing counter he downed his Tincture of Rhubarb, had a joke with my father and paid his shilling. He could have had a bottle of the stuff for the same price but he liked to be given the draught in the shop. He was not short of a penny, though, having progressed from hand-cart to Rolls-Royce. A large, cheerful soul who teased my father about his small size; in fact, his wife also teased Dad saying, 'If you get any thinner you will slip through a crack in the floor-boards.' But Dad's appetite was a healthy one and he outlived the other man by many years and enjoyed having his shop, serving the customers with 'bronical' mixtures for their 'tissicks' and deciphering the hieroglyphics on the prescriptions from various doctors as well as delivering medicines to those unable to fetch them for themselves. He dispensed compassion as well as medicines. The description of the chemist's shop in the poem, 'Miss Thompson Goes Shopping' by Martin Armstrong is very close to the reality of those days especially where he says,

'The old strange fragrance filled the air,
A fragrance like the garden pink,
But tinged with a vague medicinal stink
Of camphor, soap, new sponges blent
With chloroform and violet scent.'

Chemists' shops always had a fascinating smell compounded of dozens of different odours but there was one which swamped the rest and when we smelt *valerian* we made as quick an exit as possible; that definitely *was a medicinal stink*!

And, of course, *' . . . . . . .Brown paper, string,*
He will not use for anything,
But all in neat white parcels packs
And sticks them up with sealing wax.'

Try as I did I never mastered the art of packing as neatly as Dad and watched with admiration his deft movements as he folded the white paper and sealed it with a dab of sealing wax; the stick of sealing wax, ready for use, resting in a small tin lid near a lighted gas jet.

We were not always needed to work in the shop, of course, but it helped when one of the two assistants was on holiday. We visited friends, had day trips by train to Yarmouth or Lowestoft and we played tennis, lots of tennis. I belonged to the junior tennis club and, on one occasion played for them against Wroxham junior club. We cycled the seven miles there. I had only just been given my first bicycle, neither asked for nor wanted. I had been most ungrateful, I'm afraid, preferring to walk. Of course, I could not have walked to Wroxham, although, on the occasion I have in mind, it might have been as quick to do so. Some of the others had racing bikes and belonged to cycling clubs and would have got there in no time without me, but - my bike just would not go properly! It was terrifically hard work and my legs were like jelly by the time we arrived, later than expected. No doubt I was hopeless - I cannot remember much of the game, only the effort and embarrassment involved in getting there. As soon as possible, I made my excuses to leave and cycled home alone - amazingly quickly because the brake blocks which had, evidently, jammed on soon after setting out, freed themselves! I had been trying to cycle with the brakes *on!*

Church

A small boost came to restore my tennis ego one evening when, on the Recreation-ground courts, I retrieved a difficult back hand and heard the loud voice of the Curate, Rev. T.O.W. Glass, boom out, 'Bravo Brenda! Bravo!' I had not been aware of his presence but he, and the Vicar, Rev. Aubrey Aitken, were frequently to be seen striding about the parish visiting people or looking in on the various groups and clubs.

There were two churches in Sprowston, the ancient parish church and the more recently built St Cuthbert's which Rev. Aitken said reminded him of an upturned boat. It *was* rather like that, but my sister and I frequently went there for Evensong. The church was well attended especially when the vicar was preaching because Rev. Aitken could hold the congregation spell-bound, his strong voice reverberating in every corner of the building. Years later an operation on his throat cruelly robbed him of that voice, but, even when he had only a hoarse whisper, he continued to command the attention of everybody present. I can see him still, tall and dark, following the choir in procession and prepared to bring it to a standstill and make us start the hymn again if we were not raising the roof - or the Cross.

'Lift high the Cross!' his voice rang out, 'The love of Christ proclaim!'

He was an inspiration. We were sorry when he moved on, eventually to become Bishop of Lynn.

Matins was usually held at the old parish church of St Mary's and St Margaret's, mainly because there was no electric lighting there for Evensong. Harvest Thanksgiving was something very special, the lovely old church full and all sorts of produce displayed around, sheaves of wheat, apples, carrots, potatoes, tomatoes, everything of the best and, on gigantic marrows, candles lined up to provide light. Churchwardens were kept alert watching the candles as they spilled wax and became a fire-hazard. Many of the congregation actually did work on the land or were associated with farming or market gardening at that time. It was a service we did not want to miss.

Another annual event connected with the church was the Garden Fête held in the vicarage grounds. There must have been years when it rained but, in my memory, it was always hot and sunny. Various stalls set all around the large lawn: bowling for the pig, hoop-la, darts, bric-a-brac, guessing how many buttons on an apron, and teas. There was a sack race, an egg and spoon race, bonniest baby, knobbly knees and anything which could be thought up to make money for the church funds.

We enjoyed it all, but one year Mother wished she had not gone as she lost the gold horse-head seal which was part of a chain she had inherited. If the horse's head had landed amongst the bric-a-brac someone got a real bargain, but more likely it got lost in the long grass. We hunted for it for ages and reported the loss, but we did not see it again.

In the autumn of 1950 I was with a group receiving instruction for confirmation from the Rev.W.Aubrey Aitken and we were confirmed on 7th December at St Cuthbert's Church, Sprowston. In a specially made white dress I stood with others before the Bishop of Thetford to affirm my faith and the following Sunday accompanied my Father and Margaret to make my first communion. At Christmas there was the wonderful experience of midnight communion for the first time and that wonder has not diminished with the passing years. One year I can recall walking home after the midnight service with Mother and Margaret under a full moon while the pavements beneath our feet sparkled with frost. It was pure beauty and we were all so happy. We crept indoors so as not to wake our little sister although Dad had been waiting for us. Father Christmas had been, but we were old enough to be able to leave our pillowcases full of gifts until morning.

Having a little sister made Christmas seem extra special because we could share in her delight, and delight in her toys, too. All through the war years Father Christmas had been marvellous, finding our empty pillow cases hung at the end of our beds, even when we spent Christmas with Grandfather at Huntingdon. But in the war years he had difficulty getting books, colouring books, paints, crayons, jigsaw puzzles and toys to put in them. Often the presents were useful things such as slippers, pinafores, mittens and such-like, but one year I remember discovering a 'spectroscope', a triangular shaped tube where scraps of paper and tiny beads provided an endless variety of patterns which amused me for hours. Always we found at the bottom of our 'sack' an orange, an apple, some nuts and a brand new 10/- note from Grandfather Sayle.

Of course, we had a Christmas tree and there was great excitement when Dad brought it home and settled it into a bucketful of earth. Then out came the box of decorations, carefully stored since the previous year because there was no chance of being able to buy more during the war. Over the years they gradually reduced in number as some of the glass baubles were broken and we resorted to making decorations from all sorts of bits and pieces. Paper bells and streamers became increasingly tatty but we did not mind and, somehow, rediscovering these old friends year after year gave a sense of stability. Holly was placed on the pictures hanging from the picture rails and a little piece of mistletoe was strategically placed in the hall.

After the piano arrived, every Christmas morning started with Dad playing Christians Awake and later in the day, when, tired from all the excitement, I sat and watched the magic of the constantly flickering sparkles of colour and light from the tinsel, there were more carols, always ending with Hark the Herald, Dad's favourite.

Christmas fare, even throughout the war years, was traditional. Roast chicken was the speciality and that is how my little day-old-chicks of April 1945 ended their days that year. I did not like to think about it, but watched as they were plucked and Mother lit a twisted taper of newspaper to singe them clean of feathers. Weighing seven and a half pounds, stuffed with home-made sage and onion stuffing, the chicken was brought from the oven glistening brown, sizzling hot and delicious!

Our Christmas Pudding was always home-made, the ingredients having been carefully put aside from the rations. Some years silver threepenny pieces were washed and included in the mixture for lucky finders. One year the pudding itself was far from lucky. It was probably when I was about nine and had been busy all morning helping Mother make it. We had spent a lovely morning together in the kitchen until I lifted the large earthenware bowl from the table to transfer it to the pantry. The bowl, much heavier than I had anticipated, slipped through my hands and crashed on to the floor. I stared at the mess in horror. Mother gasped, then, seeing my woebegone face she said,

'Oh dear, Brennie. We'll have to save what we can.'

She did not scold me, but merely helped me salvage as much as possible, and was as sorry for me as for what happened. It was an accident and, as she said consolingly, accidents do happen. We had a smaller pudding than usual that year, but it is one which I shall never forget and for which my own children ought to be thankful, because Mother's reaction then

'Oh dear, Brennie...'

has helped me to be more understanding when accidents have happened in my own home.

Throughout the war, and for some years afterwards, every year the postman delivered a large parcel from Dad's cousin in South Africa. It contained all sorts of luxuries not obtainable here. There might be fruit cake, almonds and muscatels, pecan nuts and tins of pineapple, peaches and pears. They were a very welcome addition to our Christmas celebrations.

Gradually goods became more available in the shops as rationing eased. Even items such as Christmas cards had been difficult to get and it was not until the 1950s that the demand for them increased rapidly. After school, squeezing into Leveton's, the art dealers on Orford Hill, or into Hallam's in the Arcade, or Goose's or Hickling's in Davey Place, we sought out cards for our friends and posted them in boxes set up in the school.

Nothing is Perfect

We were definitely upper school pupils by the time we reached the fourth year. The geography mistress was our form mistress and geography, although a difficult subject, can be very interesting. We could not hope for full marks though, because, as our teacher explained, 'nothing is perfect in this world'! At one time I joined the school geographical society, although that was mainly because my sister did not want me to join the dramatic society as she was a member of that active body, but there was not much life in the geographical society and I cannot recall *any* outings. After the first year we had the same mistress throughout the high school but the thing I remember most clearly was not her teaching of geography, but that, like Sister Thérèse all those years before when I was in Prep. 6, she insisted that I *change my writing!* Her reason for the demand was that mine was too much like my sister's. Small and rounded, it was not actually much different from anybody else's in the form, but she wanted it altered, so, having turned the page in my exercise book, once again I sloped my writing and it has had a slope to it ever since.

School dinners had improved greatly, being cooked in the school kitchens. Each form was allocated one or two of the long polished wooden tables and sat on bentwood chairs with someone in charge at one end. A teacher supervised proceedings.

On a day when that teacher was Amblo, one of the girls at my table discovered a large caterpillar on her lettuce. Ugh! She walked up to Amblo bearing the plate of salad and pointed out the offending creature. Amblo looked at it carefully, stroked it gently, and said,

'Don't worry, it will be all right. It is still alive. Take it outside and put it in the garden.' Amblo had a soft spot for such creatures and cared for the convent bee hives.

The girl was rendered speechless. She went outside and returned without the caterpillar, no doubt hoping a hungry bird would soon discover it. She could *not* bring herself to eat the 'contaminated' salad but was not allowed a replacement lunch.

Amblo rang the little bell indicating time to finish, and 'no talking'. She issued the edict,

'Pass up!' and there was a great clattering of plates as our empty dishes

'Don't worry, it's still alive...'

were transferred to one end. Then the order came to,

'Fold up!' which always made us giggle and, instead of folding our damask napkins, we attempted to fold our own bodies

The school-leaving examinations were still a long way off and this was possibly our most relaxed year. We were growing up, too, and those of us who had always had our hair in pig-tails were experiencing short hair and the difficulties of sleeping with metal Dinkie curlers in place.

Needlework had disappeared from our time-tables and the space in our report books was given to 'deportment'. We must conduct ourselves as young ladies (even though the school no longer claimed we were such!), never seek to push ourselves forward, (which may explain why many of us are unlikely to get the bargains at jumble sales!) and, of course, respect our elders.

Outside school we were beginning to spread our wings a little. Many of us spent our Saturday afternoons learning ballroom dancing at Eileen Page's School of Dancing in Elm Hill. For the first time we experimented with lipstick and face powder. Some of the girls were envious that my father had a chemist's shop. All those lipsticks and nail varnishes to chose from, or so they thought - but it was not like that at all. The family had to make do with shop-soiled things. Not that I was particularly interested in cosmetics, but I did like to take care of my hair which was no longer in pigtails, had been cut and was being allowed to grow again. Using soft water from the rain barrel (strained through a cloth to remove the gnat larvae and pupae) I tried out the new liquid shampoos, the first of which was called White Rain. For several weeks advertising hoardings bore the slogan *'White Rain is coming- It is sweeping America now!'* and all sorts of people were speculating as to what type of commodity White Rain could possibly be. Apart from Drene, for years we had had shampoos in powder form which had to be mixed before use. And there were *dry* shampoos to use during *those special days* of the month when it was considered *unwise* for young women to shampoo their hair! Just at the very time when a shampoo seemed highly desirable, an old wives' tale still held sway. As a little girl *no one* can have made more fuss than I when having my hair washed, but there comes a time when children reach a self-awareness and take a pride in their appearance. I spent hours in the bathroom shampooing my locks, rinsing them thoroughly in water to which a little vinegar or lemon juice had been added and then kneeling in front of the fire to dry them, brushing and brushing to make my hair shine. Incidentally, about this time, Dad gave me a hairbrush, the bristles of which were *whalebone.* A commercial traveller had given him a sample - a new use for whalebone. It was not very satisfactory and did not last for long. I am ashamed to say I do not recall any feeling of guilt that whales were killed to provide such items. Instead, we heard with pride how brave the men were who sailed in the whalers. It was the same when I was given some turtle-oil soap. For a long time I did not consider how or why the turtles died. But these were times when every woman longed for a real fur coat, mink, leopard, ocelot, silver fox or whatever. Royalty wore them, the glamorous film stars wore them, and they looked wonderful. No one seems to have thought of the animals.

Sometimes we met our friends in Norwich and went to the Pictures and saw the Hollywood stars flaunting their beautiful fur coats. But it was the male film stars who were most likely to capture our teenage hearts. It must have been about this time that I first saw Gregory Peck as Captain Horatio Hornblower. Gregory Peck, if any film star did, was the one who made me feel weak. Inside many desk lids at school were pictures of Dirk Bogarde, Trevor Howard, Rock Hudson, Kirk Douglas and any hero who could provide inspiration when needed. They sometimes had success when our prayers did not.

Proof that prayers *could* work was made clear to me at the time of the

Festival of Britain in 1951. The teachers were telling us that we ought to go. Teachers were often saying we should get our parents to take us to see various things such as, at one time, the herring fleet at Lowestoft because we ought to watch the Scottish fisher-girls working. But, like many others, my parents could not take us, in spite of our pleadings. There was no chance that I would be taken to the Festival and I did so want to go. In bed, near to tears, I prayed and prayed that somehow I might get to see it. Incredibly, the next day, the mother of my friend Vivien telephoned asking if I would like to go with them. I could not believe my luck.

The day came and we went to London. I had never seen so many people and there were queues to get in to every part of the exhibition. We went in to the huge Dome of Discovery and I was horrified when Vivien volunteered to be one of the people standing against the wall encircling the floor of the Rotordrome; the whole thing rotated and, when at high speed the floor lowered away from their feet, they *stuck to the wall*! No one would have got me on that thing! Outside, the Skylon was an eye-catching piece of engineering, seeming to hang in space; graceful, inspiring and memorably beautiful. People were enjoying rides on the fascinating, fairytale-like Emmett Railway. There was so much to see, so many people to wait behind or squeeze past and too little time to see it all, but at least I *had* been there, seen something of it and *was satisfied*.

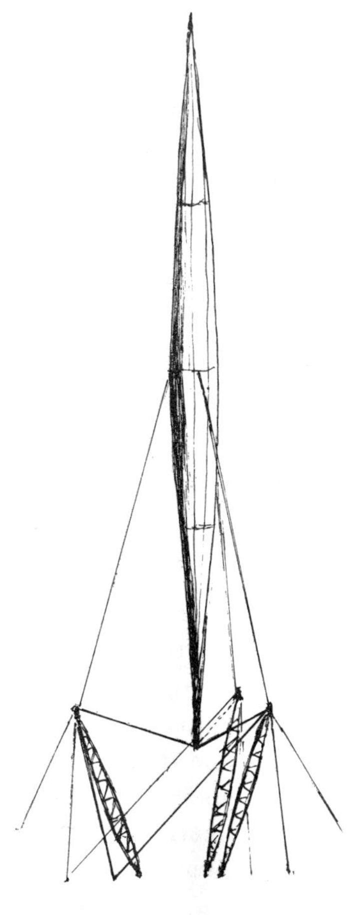

The Skylon, described in the official souvenir book as 'a vertical feature in steel and aluminium by Powell and Moya'.

Looking to the Future

When we were in Form I the girls of the fifth form had seemed very superior. We knew most of the names of girls senior to us as we looked up to them. All too soon *we* were fifth formers ourselves and embarking on the most serious year of study because, at the end of it, we would sit the General Certificate of Education at Ordinary Level. The Advanced Level Examinations would be taken after two years in the sixth form. Unfortunately, as I have already mentioned, for myself and two of my friends this year would *not* be when we sat our O-Levels because we were *too young*; our birthdays came after September 1st and we would have to wait another year. Even so we felt the pressure as the year progressed.

Every year throughout the school we had set books for English including at least one Shakespeare play. Large passages were learned by heart. For one of our rare school outings we were taken to the pictures to see Laurence Olivier as Henry V. There were other plays such as *The Rivals* and *She Stoops to Conquer* as well as some Chaucer. There was poetry, too, to commit to memory - *Hyperion, Sohrab and Rustum, St Agnes' Eve, Michael* and many more. *Silas Marner* was read and re-read and analysed in detail.

Other subjects were equally demanding, French, history, geography, scripture, Latin, mathematics, biology, but unfortunately there was no longer room on the time-table for art. Several of us wanted to do art, but the so-called 'academic' subjects took precedence. Always having enjoyed art, I was more than a little disappointed. The art mistress who had taught us in the earlier years had left, but I still treasure the pencil drawing of a wild poppy which she made in my autograph book and many may remember her arriving at school wearing the New Look for the first time. After the drab, skimpy clothes of war-time she certainly caused many heads to turn when walking down the road, her full brilliant-orange skirt swirling almost to her ankles. Reaching an age of fashion awareness, our imaginations were stirred.

Early in 1952 the whole country was mourning the death of King George VI. The announcement was made during the school day and many of the girls dissolved into tears at the news. King George and Queen Elizabeth had been a source of stability and unity throughout the war years. Now we would have a young Queen with a handsome Prince and their young family. When the shock of the King's death had passed, it was exciting to realise we were in a New Elizabethan Age.

The weeks of the first term in Form V rushed by. There was all the extra work associated with 'Black Baby Day', the annual bazaar, when money raised was given to overseas nuns to help in their caring work. The Dramatic Society put on a play which always received great acclaim. The splendid scenery was made by the school carpenter/caretaker and painted by the Art department. One year, nothing less than Dido and Aeneas was performed, the beautiful voice of Barbara Stringer receiving special mention in the local press. Then all of us were singing, practising carols and more carols for Christmas. Christmas or not we were given homework for the holidays and warned that when we returned the pressure really would be on and the examinations would rush in on us.

It must have been about this time that we were asked which careers we wished to follow. No teacher was especially designated as career mistress and we were asked, almost casually, what we planned to do. Most of us had some idea, university or teacher training college, nurse, physiotherapist, secretary or something else. We all felt sure of a job because unemployment was practically unheard of and everyone knew that, should they not get a job straight away, almost certainly the Norwich Union Insurance Society would absorb them into its vast offices. Previously, for as long as I could remember, when anybody had asked me what I wanted to be when I grew up I would reply without hesitation, 'a nurse'. But now that the question had more relevance, for the first time I was, like many other teenagers, uncertain as to the way forward. Incidentally, the term 'teenager' had not been long in use. Previously one was either a child or an adolescent. Only when the school-leaving age went up did people need to find a name for teenagers - at one time, I believe, the term 'sophisticates' was even considered.

Then, one day, when assisting in my father's shop a thought entered my head, should I be a chemist? It seemed such a shame that there was no-one to take over from him when he grew older. Ought I to try? Could I do it? Tentatively I voiced my thoughts. Dad's first reaction was not really enthusiastic as he knew I had always wanted to do nursing, but on our next visit to Grandfather he mentioned the subject and, before I knew where I was, Grandfather had written to the Pharmaceutical Society for details of entry requirements. In any case, I could not take O-levels until July 1953, so there was plenty of time to make up my mind. It was quite clear that it would be better for me to stay in Form V for another year rather than move up with my own year and try to take O-levels from the Sixth form. It also became apparent that Notre Dame High School would not be able to provide all the subjects required at A-level as there was no physics laboratory and the four subjects, botany, zoology, chemistry *and* physics were needed. Norwich City College was the place to go for these when the time came.

In the meantime, work was becoming increasingly harder and my reports reflected this. Also the fact that, for me, the examinations would not take place at the end of the year, removed the driving force. It was as well that I would have another year. Biology was still my best subject and, for the first time, history was becoming interesting as we learned about social changes, the Industrial and Agrarian Revolutions. The War of the Austrian Succession had gone on for far too long! We did not get anywhere near to recent history although the very recent World War II was still affecting our lives.

It was not until 1953 that rationing finally ended. After ten and a half years of a ration allowing only about two ounces per week (it varied from time to time), sweets were coming off the ration on February 4th. For a time people went wild as they bought as many sweets as possible - much to the concern of dentists! After school there would be a rush to get to Lorraine's sweet shop in Brigg Street where, inevitably, there was a long queue - but we were used to queuing. The shop assistants became red in the face working under such pressure as most of the sweets had to be weighed out, Sherbet Lemons, Buttered Brazils, Hazelnut Creams, Richmond Selection, Sharpe's Toffees, Nuthall's Mintoes, Aniseed Balls, Pear Drops, Fox's Glacier Mints, Needler's Glacé Fruits and many more. There were bars of chocolate, coconut-ice and nougat and, before long, came the first of the ready-wrapped and packaged sweets, Spangles, hard, clear, fruit flavoured and square. The demand was so great confectioners had difficulty maintaining supplies, but it was to be expected after so many years of deprivation.

Another thing which had been out of the question was travel, especially travel abroad, and I was fortunate to be able to join a party of girls from the upper school on the school's first trip to the Continent travelling to Brussels by way of the Dover to Ostend Ferry. We stayed at the Notre Dame Convent in the Rue du Petit Potêt in Brussels which was a boarding school, although the dormitory in which we slept must have been for the smaller children as the bunk-type beds were too short for many of us! Another shock was the lack of plumbing which meant water jugs and bowls for washing and the water was *cold* and came complete with gnat larvae! And, of course, there were differences at the dining table. No cups of tea but *bowls* of strong coffee and, when we turned up our noses at spinach for a vegetable we found it proffered the next day as spinach topping on potato pie! Obviously the nuns in the kitchen knew how to overrule fussy children. Brussels, of course, was fascinating (especially, its famous fountain) and we were taken on coach trips to several places including Namur, the main convent of Notre Dame, and Dinard and a former concentration camp. With the war so fresh in our minds, this last place left us in sombre mood. For children who had not been able to travel *anywhere* the trip was a real eye-opener and we were very grateful to have had the opportunity denied to others. The Headmistress, Sister Marie, and another nun accompanied us.

Even less adventurous outings were few and far between but, after Sister Marie had discovered to her horror that most of us knew *nothing* of the famous Shrine of Our Lady at Walsingham in North Norfolk, one memorable day we were taken there by coach. During the year when Margaret was Head Girl, there were special celebrations connected with the Virgin Mary when the whole school processed through the convent grounds singing,

'Bring flowers of the rarest, bring blossoms the fairest
From garden and woodland and hillside and dale . . . .'

And many of our gardens had been stripped of any available flowers for the occasion, not without a few misgivings by some of our parents. Mother said it reminded her of when, as a young girl in 1912, she had seen the procession for the dedication of the new Roman Catholic Cathedral of St John, built on the site of the old Norwich Gaol at the top of St Giles Hill. She recalled children strewing lovely little posies of flowers in front of the procession and how she desperately wanted to rescue the beautiful blooms from being trampled underfoot by a 'lot of fat old men'! I don't think any of *our* flowers were trampled upon during our procession as we stood in the shade of the large trees around the grass tennis courts and chorused,

'Welcome month of Mary!'

It was very impressive. All the hours of singing rehearsal to satisfy

Miss Cocks paid off and we were well satisfied, just as we had been a year earlier when the Mother Superior of the Order of Notre Dame came from Namur to visit us. It must have been to celebrate the bicentenary of the birth of the founder of the order, Marie Julie Billiart, in 1751. For weeks beforehand we practised, *'Praise to the Lord, the Almighty, the King of Cre. .a. . a. . a . .tion!'* until it was perfect and Miss Cocks must have suffered nightmares in the process.

Whilst our class were sitting O-levels the three of us too young to do so felt very left out. We had to attend school but nobody wanted us. We soon tired of reading and were pleased to be able to help Sister Theresa of the Holy Name who was in charge of the book store. In the windowless cupboard which smelled strongly of beeswax candles, we covered scores of books with brown paper until supplies of paper ran out. It was lovely weather and we lazed away our days playing tennis on the grass courts in the convent grounds and sitting in the shade of the big trees, chatting about anything and everything until even our chatter dried up.

Eventually the examinations were over. Last day of term came - the last day of school for some. Photographs were taken on Brownie Box cameras and tears were shed, especially when we all went in to the Assembly Hall and sang the School Song,

'Mother of all that is pure and good, all that is bright and blest,
As we have taken our toil to thee, so will we take our rest.
Take now and bless our holiday.
O causa nostrae laetitiae!'

It was a most emotional day. Several hoped to return to the sixth form but many were leaving. It was like parting with family. So great was the bonding of the form over the five years that *thirty to forty* years later annual reunions brought together about half of us every time and more would have attended if they could.

Until even our chatter dried up.

A Most Important Lesson

For the first few weeks after the eight-week long summer holidays school seemed strange. Many of our friends were, of course, no longer there and those who remained were now in the sixth form with a common room and classrooms of their own. The two of us who were staying in the fifth year felt out of place - we could not be with our own group and we were intruders in the form below us. For a long time we sensed isolation although, possibly, the girls in our new class might not have realised that.

It was a very different class from ours, they were noisier, livelier, more worldly-wise and readier to 'play-up' the mistresses than ever we had been. And, as we had so often been told, they were better at mathematics than we were, but at least we were getting a second year going over some of the same work. Each form, each group of girls, living, working and playing together over five years develops its own distinctive character and we were very aware of the differences at first, but gradually we were accepted. It was not that this form was unfriendly, but we were not their members. Our form mistress was none other than Amblo!

In February the previous year, 1952, had come the shock of the death of King George VI. In 1953 there was another tragedy which resulted in hundreds of deaths, namely, the East Coast Floods. Such devastation was difficult to visualise, but we were aware that if the sea got through at Yarmouth it could come all the way to Norwich. It was frightening, even to us twenty to thirty miles inland.

But in June the Coronation was *the* spectacle to beat all other ceremonies and, just as in 1947 the whole school had been lined up in ranks and marched down Surrey Street into All Saints' Green to the Carlton Picture House to watch in colour the wedding of H.R.H. Princess Elizabeth and Lieutenant Philip Mountbatten, so in 1953, just one week after the event, we were taken en masse to see the film of the Coronation. Incredible pageantry! A sight to remember for ever.

And, throughout all the excitements taking place in the outside world, in school our learning continued unabated. Amblo took us for religious studies and Latin and it was during a Latin lesson that we learned an important lesson for life. Fifteen-year-old girls in the nineteen fifties were, on the whole, innocent. We were not expected to know the facts of life.

Discussing the really important issues

Certainly no adult discussed them with us. It was a taboo subject.

There was a time when the plaque by the main entrance door to Notre Dame High School bore the inscription 'Notre Dame High School for young ladies' but this had been adjusted several years before I entered the school. Evidently a teacher overheard a group of pupils discussing babies, where they came from and, presumably, how they got there! Disgusted that the pupils no longer qualified to be referred to as young ladies, the girls were disciplined and their parents warned that such behaviour in future would lead to their children being expelled from the school. The last three words on the plaque were discreetly obliterated.

However, girls in their second and third years still stood in little groups around the edge of the playground discussing the really important issues affecting their lives as they grew up. There was always someone who knew more than the rest. Of course, some girls were above such basic conversation and could be seen practising netball or tennis whilst the more academic might stroll round wearing a learned expression apparently reading poetry, Latin or Greek.

In a single sex school one of the biggest crimes we could commit was to be seen in the company of a boy. Not having any brothers and long since having lost contact with the boys I had known at Ebenezer House, I was really embarrassed when a ginger-haired young man who travelled on the same 'bus as myself took an interest in me. I dreaded him sitting next to me and tried to pretend he wasn't there. What a relief if he felt obliged to give up his seat for a lady passenger! Unfortunately he discovered that I still took music lessons with Miss Bidewell on a Saturday morning and was waiting for me when I came out.

Trying to pretend he wasn't there

'I've been waiting an hour for you,' he declared one day.

'That's your look out!' I responded as I flounced past him.

How cruelly can females treat the male ego! It was the only way I knew to discourage him and after that he did not aim to sit next to me on the 'bus but still stole sidelong glances when he passed by.

It was not until our fifth year that the syllabus included any education about males and females. Until then, only in our French lessons was there any reference to male and female, le and la. Biology was the obvious lesson in which to mention the subject. Our biology mistress had married and remained on the teaching staff. We continued to call her by her maiden name and, much to her embarrassment emphasised the 'Miss' when we greeted her arrival in the laboratory as her pregnancy developed. She abandoned her requests for us to use her married name and wrote on the blackboard:-

THE REPRODUCTIVE CYCLE OF THE RABBIT

There followed diagrams and notes which we duly copied. Eventually, red in the face, our teacher declared, 'That concludes the way reproduction occurs in animals. It is the same in humans!'

The same in humans! That was the sum total of our sex education. The end of session bell rang throughout the school much to the relief of Miss ...er ...Mrs.......!

'Good morning, Miss....'

In a Catholic environment one would not expect any mention of contraception, but in society generally it was not mentioned either. The safest method was to use two letters, N and O. NO! After I was fourteen some of my school holidays were spent helping in my father's Chemist's shop. Especially on Friday nights men would slip into the shop and, on seeing me behind the counter, would quietly ask if they might have a word with Mr Sayle. I relayed the request and a whispered conversation took place by the dispensing counter. A small plain brown envelope, sometimes two, would be given to the customer and my father instructed me to 'Take half-a-crown'... or 'Take five shillings from the gentleman'. Obviously it was all something to do with what went on between married men and women, but, even if, bursting with curiosity, I had asked for an explanation, it is doubtful if a satisfying answer would have been given. Such things were not spoken about.

Incredibly it was in a Latin lesson during my second year in Form V that we received further instruction about the greatest hazard waiting for us in the outside world and, as I have said, Amblo was our form mistress and our Latin mistress. Our set book was *The Odes of Horace Book III*. Valiantly Amblo struggled to instil in us a feeling for the beauty of the language but it mostly passed over our heads. We laboured over Ode 2 on 'endurance'.

'Angustam amice pauperium pati
robustus acri militia puer
condiscat'

Times had not changed! With Amblo's guidance we struggled to translate it to:-

'Let the youth hardened by active service
learn to bear trying hardships'

Latin was a trying hardship! Soon we reached the famous line:-

'Dulce et decorum est pro patria mori'
'Tis sweet and glorious to die for the fatherland'

And so it went on, lesson after lesson with Amblo attempting to kindle a spark of enthusiasm in us for her beloved Latin. To us it was all so dull until, that is, one afternoon when we reached Ode 6, an Ode on Religion and Purity. It did not look promising as wearily we opened our books unaware that we were about to hear an unforgettable lesson. Verse 5 -

'Fecunda culpae saccula nuptias
primum inquinavere et genus et domos'

Amblo must have been prepared for the reaction as we slowly translated:-

'Teeming with sin our times have sullied
first the marriage bed, our offspring and our homes'

There was an audible silence whilst our minds coped with what had been revealed. Girls surreptitiously turned their heads to grimace at each other and mouth 'the marriage bed?' For the first time Horace was getting undivided attention. The translation progressed,

'The maiden ....trains herself in coquetry ....and plans unholy amours, with passion unrestrained'.

Our pent up laughter was almost unrestrained. We moved on to verse 7 -

'soon midst her husband's revels she seeks younger paramours'.

With bated breath we waited for the meaning of

'neque eliget cui donet impermissa raptim gaudia luminibus remotis'.

Amblo was already aware of the titters, the glances and sniggers around the classroom. Her eyes were flashing warnings that she would not tolerate disruption. Her voice was becoming louder.

'nor stops to choose on whom she swiftly shall bestow illicit joys when lights are dimmed.'

Amblo decided the time had come for a lecture on moral values. She suddenly tapped her hand sharply on the desk. We jerked upright, trying hard to keep straight faces.

'Now children!' she started, her voice falling and rising as she emphasised the 'children'. 'You must realise this is not the way to behave. The young woman was making eyes at her husband's guests when the lights were low!' Amblo was getting rather red in the face, her eyes filling with water as she surveyed the giggling girls before her.

'Now children! I have something very important to say to you. Sit up and listen.'

'Now children'

We tried to sober down. The nun looked from one to another of us all round the room whilst we waited tentatively.

'Now children you are all reaching a most attractive age and will soon be leaving school and working side by side with . . . ', she paused, her eyes flashing round the room. There was not a sound, you could have heard a pin drop. We held our breath and waited for her to continue. With great emphasis she enunciated 'working side by side with . . . *MARRIED MEN!'*

Stifled laughter shook the class. Married men were not to be trusted and best avoided at all times. Obviously Amblo was genuinely concerned for us, knowing how innocent and unprepared we were for the big wide world. We had been very sheltered until now.

Somehow we worked our way through to the end of the ode. Eventually the bell rang for the end of the lesson; Amblo gathered up her books and left the classroom which immediately erupted into mirthful chatter. It was incredible that a nun and Quintus Horatius Flaccus born in 65BC provided sex education for the 20th century - but the ways of the world had not changed.

This year flew by even quicker than the last one and there came the dreaded day when we filed in to the Assembly Hall, sat at individual tables and read the first of many examination papers to be placed before us between the 6th and the 18th of July. Not a sound could be heard apart from the scratching of busy pens and the occasional sigh. Naturally some papers were better than expected, some a lot worse. My most stressful day was when there was a mathematics paper in the morning, a Latin paper in the afternoon and then, when utterly exhausted, I had to go for a music examination as my music teacher (no longer Miss Bidewell) had entered me for one. Rushing out of school I hurried as fast as my legs would cover the two miles (or thereabouts) to the Baptist Church along St Benedict's Street where the music examinations were held. The sight of the bulky red-brick building caused my heart to sink. I was only just in time but my teacher was there. Summoned in I sat before the unfamiliar piano and my mind went blank. The scale of C sharp minor? What was this man asking? My fingers fumbled the keys but, eventually, I recovered enough in time to play Haydn's Gipsy Rondo and another piece and somehow scraped a pass. It was an experience I never wanted to repeat.

Soon the last day of term was upon us - the last day of school for many. There was the usual cleaning of desks, the pungent aroma of polish and vinegar, the school assembly and the singing of the emotive school song. Many of the girls were crying their eyes out but, when I went to collect my report book and say goodbye to Amblo, she looked at me quizzically,

'What no tears, Brenda?' she asked.

I shook my head, 'No, Sister!' and failed to conceal my joy. The broadest of grins spread across my face. I had waited a long time for this day, although I never discovered what it was about school which made me feel sick before the start of each term and so happy on the last day.

During the following holiday the day came when we went to the school to discover our O-Level results. Nervously I rang the door bell and was taken to the Headmistress's Office. Her first remark was encouraging,

'Well done for your English!' Sister Marie smiled at me.

Well, that was a pleasant surprise! Biology had always been my best subject, but I had done better at English literature than expected. However, I had got biology and mathematics, English language, French, and history, but sadly I had only obtained a grade 6 for geography and Latin, not quite good enough to pass.

'Pity about the Latin, Brenda!' remarked Amblo as she opened the door to let me out. Yes, it was a pity, and I feel sure if she had taught me from the start the result might have been a happier one. However, my results were sufficient to take me on to the next step and I could enrol for the science course at Norwich City College.

Norwich City College

All through the war a large skeleton of iron girders stood beside the Ipswich Road in Norwich. Unlike the iron railings outside the hundreds of terrace houses and around parks and gardens these girders were not taken away to make bombs for the war effort but stood, waiting optimistically, as a monument to the future. They were the framework for the new Technological College. The old one in St George's Street was cramped for space. As soon as the war ended, optimism was rewarded and work started on the building of what was to be known internationally as Norwich City College.

Early in September 1953 I made my way to that large building and enrolled for the necessary subjects. Term started on 14th September. To enter that world after all those years at school was like being set free from a cage. The place and much of the equipment was new; there were hundreds and hundreds of people; there were girls and women, men and boys, many overseas students, mainly from Asia and Africa; we were treated like adults instead of children; lectured rather than taught and the atmosphere of the whole place was vibrant and stimulating.

One of our first lectures took place in the chemistry laboratory. I shared a work bench with a girl from Uganda. Hazilda was sixteen, the same age as myself, but she had travelled all the way from Uganda *alone!* And I had never been *anywhere*; even a 'bus trip to King's Lynn had been a major adventure! I was very impressed. We became good friends and are still in touch over forty years later.

Science, being a speciality which attracted more males than females, girls were much in the minority. However, at times, that proved an advantage because, before the feminist movement and equality of the sexes, the young men *would not dream* of letting mere girls struggle to carry heavy weights needed for physics experiments, for example. In fact, the lecturer would volunteer one of the class - possibly attempting a bit of match-making in the process.

'Who will offer to carry these weights upstairs for Miss . .?' his voice would boom out across the practical room.

Usually several hands would go up and the lecturer then turned to the embarrassed girl,

'Take your pick, Miss . . . ' and, if she hesitated, he might suggest someone, 'How about T . . . - he is good to look at!' Undoubtedly the girl would blush and shyness descend on the young man in question as he struggled with the heavy load. The lecturer thought it all rather amusing. In time we were less embarrassed by such incidents as we quickly adapted to co-educational existence.

Maybe I felt at home at Norwich City College more easily than I had expected, but unfortunately I also rapidly realised that the work was far above me, especially chemistry and physics. To be thrown into A-level work without the barest of basics was disastrous. Chemistry caused the greatest anguish and the lecturer shook his head as he regarded my work, his voice not able to disguise his feelings of despair, but how was I to know that a white salt sitting on a crucible open to the air could not be a copper salt? Neither did I realise that I must check the fume cupboard fan was working before starting work there, and, if it had not been for a quick thinking fellow student, I might well have succumbed to hydrogen sulphide! In truth, I just did not know the most base of basics. I should not have been accepted on to the A-level course, but I had been assured that the lectures would cover the basics during the first half term, and had imagined that, provided I worked hard, I would be able to catch up. Until then I had foolishly thought that anyone can do anything if they put their mind to it, but I could not work *that* hard and by half-term had discovered my limitations. My presence in chemistry lectures was a waste of the lecturer's and my own time. And, of course, without chemistry I could not consider pharmacy as a career. My father was not unduly surprised or disappointed, but it was more difficult breaking the news to Grandfather.

Nursing was clearly the path to follow, but as the minimum age for entry to a School of Nursing was eighteen years I continued on the science course, minus chemistry, until the end of the academic year.

I continued with physics although not much better at it than at chemistry, again lacking previous tuition in the subject and not being *brilliant* at mathematics. We did, in fact, have one afternoon of mathematics-for-scientists squeezed in to our crowded time-table. There were, however, a few aspects of physics which I enjoyed and understood, 'light' being one of them. The lecturer smiled wryly as he dispatched pairs of students to dark rooms to experiment. In those innocent days there was no need to expect that anything other than work took place in the dark rooms. I remember spending one afternoon shut in a dark room with a student from Ceylon (as Sri Lanka was then named) and, I must confess, I was nervous; maybe he was too. He was very good looking although all I could see in the dark were his teeth and the whites of his eyes. I wonder what Amblo would have thought! If I understood a little about light it was a different story with mechanics. I had never heard of pile drivers, the worm and wheel or screw jacks. The practical sessions were a discovery of possible disasters.

We were given a welcome break during the three-hour practicals and made our way quickly to the canteen in a wooden hut at the back of the college where we bought cups of coffee or tea and chocolate Penguin biscuits, a delicious newcomer to the canteen supplies. Our break lasted not more than fifteen minutes, but one day that was long enough for my return to be greeted by an irate lecturer bawling,

'Miss Sayle! Sixty pounds worth of damage!'

I stopped dead in my tracks and stared at him in horror. What had I done? I had been doing some experiment on Charles' Law or Boyle's Law or some such and it was not something I *had* done but rather something I *had not* done and the mercury was flowing towards *somewhere it ought not to be*. Fortunately, *very* fortunately for me, the lecturer had seen what was happening and saved the day!

'Sixty pounds worth of damage you might have caused if I had not noticed it!'

There were no such problems in the botany and zoology laboratories. We had studied biology at school although we had not worked with microscopes and this especially appealed to me. In zoology we dissected small creatures and animals which was interesting although not for the squeamish. I enjoyed zoology, but much preferred botany.

Whatever the subject, we welcomed any lecturer whose idiosyncracies enlivened a difficult session. The most reliable of these was a tall, somewhat round-shouldered gentleman with greying hair which flopped in a small clump over his forehead, eagle eyes peering from behind horn-rimmed spectacles, and large outstanding ears. Silently he would enter the classroom exactly one minute before the lesson was due to begin. Any student entering after him was greeted with a loud 'It's a good thing we don't pay you by the hour!' or some similar pleasantry. When more late-comers drifted in he became obviously annoyed and a triumphant smile flashed over his face as he deliberately strode across the room and locked the door. No more intruders!

He would call the register in an alternately loud and quiet voice taking great pride in the pronunciation of long and difficult Siamese names. One day the calling of a Nigerian name resulted in total class hysteria as he boomed the surname 'Mama' and the student answered, 'Yes Papa!' The lecturer joined in our laughter which took several minutes to subside.

Glaring round at the eager - *eager?* - faces before him he would take a deep breath and the lesson began with a booming sentence, a tone probably adopted for the benefit of those who had drowsed into a state of semiconscious bliss since answering to their names. They awoke to find some questions illegibly written on the blackboard and a stentorian voice inviting them to 'Rack your brains on those!'

Having come to terms with failing and no longer trying to cope with chemistry I relaxed more and enjoyed my year at college. It was a good place to be; everybody was friendly and we had a lot of fun. Midday meals were available in the canteen although we tried to avoid the crush in there and headed instead for the superior dining room serviced by the Catering School. The Catering School was becoming well known for its excellence and we sampled that excellence for a mere three shillings for a three-course meal and an extra threepence for coffee. When we could not afford such luxury we dashed in to the city to the Clover Leaf Café in Dove Street where we could get a two-course meal of, say, fish and chips and peas, followed by jam tart and custard for only one shilling and sixpence! Enough - but a frantic rush to get back in time for the afternoon's lectures.

Staff and students who had fond memories of the old Tech. missed the friendly family atmosphere of that place but the new City College soon developed its own atmosphere. Thursday afternoons were given over to sport, there were dances, plays and concerts in the main hall and the corridors and stairways echoed to people singing or whistling the waltz tune from *The Moulin Rouge*. I remember deciding to have my hair cut short - quite a decision to make as, for a long time, I had had a pony-tail which bounced up and down as I stepped out and caused wolf-whistles from passing lorry drivers (but, having been to Notre Dame, I took no apparent notice, of course) and the male students were sorry there was no longer a pony tail to pull! The mother of one of my friends was a hairdresser and the current style was a D.A. (a 'Duck's Arse' - because that was the shape of it) but it did not stay that shape on me as my hair was of the wrong texture.

During the spring holidays we went on a biology foray to the Lake District. We stayed in cottages at Clappersgate, a small village near Ambleside and went on various forays in the area. I, for one, had never seen such scenery or ever climbed such hills. Sheep and lambs were all about, wandering across roads and by streams. We fished for plankton in Lake Windermere, one of the Nigerian boys almost overturning the boat in his enthusiasm. We peered at our findings through microscopes when safely on dry land. On a very warm day we set out, haversacks bulging with packed lunches, prepared for a long walk in the Langdale Valley. The coach stopped at a farm and we set off with enthusiasm but, before long, Hazilda and I had decided enough was enough and we did not go over the top with the rest. We spent a most enjoyable afternoon in the valley and bottle fed some orphan lambs on the farm. The hours passed and still no sign of our friends. We knew they would not have lost their way as our Head of Science, Mr Jones, was with them and he knew the area well. Eventually, small figures appeared on the hill-top and wearily they made their way to us, scarcely able to put one foot in front of the other. They had been walking and climbing for about ten hours. One of the Ghanaian boys could scarcely take another step, but somehow managed to reply 'Yes. Lovely!' when the farmer called out 'Lovely day!' as he reached the coach in a state of exhaustion. His face was drained and his smile a weak effort compared to his usual broad grin, but he had managed to complete the course and, tired and happy, could look back on the day with satisfaction. Everyone was too tired to talk and the coach was abnormally quiet as we were taken back to Clappersgate. All too soon we had to return to Norfolk and college, better for the experience and closer as a group.

Back at college work continued to increase. I was glad I had dropped chemistry as there was enough to do without that and the nine to five intensive brain work was tiring. We were glad when work finished for the day and we could join the throng leaving the building. In front of the college main entrance the few cars belonging to staff members were parked. Some of the staff cycled and all the students, who did not walk or use public transport, cycled. Just after 5 p.m. a river of cyclists poured from the college grounds and flowed down Ipswich Road along St Stephen's Road, past the Norfolk and Norwich Hospital and spread through the city.

Every day as I walked past the Norfolk and Norwich Hospital I thought about my future and nursing. I really knew very little about hospitals and was not sure where I would like to train. I wrote to the King Edward Fund for Nursing and received a helpful reply listing various hospitals in London, Oxford, Cambridge and Norwich. The Norfolk and Norwich was held in high regard and, during the war, great praise had been heaped upon the matron and her staff. The National Health Service had been introduced in 1948 and there was a new matron, reputed to be very strict, but nearly all matrons had that reputation. The sister of one of my college friends was nearing the completion of her training to be a nurse at the Norfolk and Norwich and, I gathered, had found it hard work. She confirmed the rumours about the matron being something of a 'dragon', and evidently not the only one to her mind, but perhaps she was exaggerating. I hoped she was. At any rate, she had survived, so . . . why not me?

In spite of the disappointments I had experienced at college it had been a good year; a very memorable one; making friends, male and female; a time for feeling free and getting a glimpse of the greater world. After the sheltered atmosphere of the Notre Dame High School it *had* felt like being set free from a cage to go to the College, yet now I was voluntarily considering entering another cage. However, if I wanted to be a nurse, and I did, cages and dragons must not deter me.

I plucked up courage and wrote to the matron.

'Is This You, Nurse?'

by Brenda Sayle

tells the story of the author's experiences as a nurse in the Norwich hospitals during the 'fifties.

Also available from the Larks Press - price £6.95.